CONTENTS

Preface 4
Willy Russell's Introduction to this Edition 5
Educating Rita 7
Experiencing a Play: Suggestions 79

Additional Material
Non-fictional Texts

1. Lern Yerself Scouse. How to talk proper in Liverpool 81
2. Does Accent Matter? The Pygmalion Factor 83
3. The Open University 84
4. Willy Russell, Educating the Author 93
5. Educating Lisa 99
6. Folk Tale from Liverpool 100
7. Twenty Years of Willy Russell 102
8. Interview with Willy Russell (9 March 1982) 103
9. Interview with Willy Russell (16 October 1996) 105
10. A Touch of Working Class 113
11. Substance, Wit and Style Characterize Performance 115

Fictional Texts (excerpts)

1. Bernard Shaw, Pygmalion 117
2. Arnold Wesker, Roots 129
3. Charles Dickens, Hard Times 130
4. Thomas Hughes, Tom Brown's School Days 131
5. Muriel Spark, The Prime of Miss Jean Brodie 132
6. Charles Causley, Timothy Winters 132
7. Barry Hines, Kes 133
8. Walt Whitman, When I Heard the Learn'd Astronomer 135

Century Theatre presents:

Educating Rita (Cartoon) 136

PREFACE

This annotated edition of *Educating Rita* is a revised and updated version of the edition published in 1984. It contains not only the play, but also additional texts which provide factual knowledge and background information. This can also help to contextualise *Educating Rita* by comparing the play with other literary texts and stageplays, in particular Shaw's *Pygmalion.* The impact which Willy Russell's play has had on audiences and readers since it was first produced in the early eighties is reflected in articles, reviews and a recent interview (October 1996), in which the author articulates his view of the relevance of *Educating Rita* in the late nineties.
Theatres, students and teachers have approached this play in various ways, which is exactly what Willy Russell likes to see being done. There is, indeed, no one approach or rationale, there are no definitive answers. The hints given on page 79–80 in this edition are merely suggestions to help those readers who have so far not had any experience in dealing with a text that was primarily written to be played. What the dramatist wrote in the introduction to the 1984 edition has still not lost any of its relevance: "Watch and listen to the play – it contains all its own answers." In the interview which I conducted with him especially for this new edition the author went a step further:

> I wanted to write a play in such a way that my mother, an uneducated woman, could enjoy the play without feeling intimidated by the names [in it. And] it is written in such a way that with no knowledge of, no understanding of English literature, or reference points with which to connect things like *Howards End,* the poetry of William Blake, the Beat Poets, William Shakespeare, you could still unterstand what they represent, because you understand through Rita's eyes.

Here's the play – enjoy!

A.R.G

WILLY RUSSELL'S INTRODUCTION

It's now more than a year since Albert-Reiner Glaap asked me to write an introduction for his edition of my play *Educating Rita*. He asked me simply to write some background to the piece, and so why has it taken me so long? Well, I don't like writing *about* my plays; I like writing them but not *about* them. This is not because I am too busy or lazy or insecure (although, of course, I am all of these) but rather because if my plays are of any value they must walk and stand and live alone, unaided by any rationale I might provide.

I write my plays to be played, not to be studied; if that sounds ungrateful let me add that I don't object to studying the plays, but they are not primarily written for this; for a playwright the medium is the performance whilst the book is merely a record of the text.

So, the most honest and valid thing I can say to anyone studying *Educating Rita* is watch and listen to the play – it contains all its own answers. I've never liked plays which, in order to be understood, require a greater degree of information than that contained in the play itself. Such plays, with their footnotes and comments are usually pieces of propaganda, masquerading as drama or historical relics best left on the library shelf or impenetrable examples of the latest new wave which attract the attention of the critic but rarely that of the audience.

Even though *Educating Rita* is in part about literature, language and education, I wanted to make a play which engaged and was relevant to those who had no knowledge of literature, those who considered themselves uneducated, those whose daily language is not the language of the university or the theatre. In short I wanted to write a play which would attract, and be as valid for, the *Ritas* in the audience as well as the *Franks* and the *Trishs*. I think (I certainly hope) that the play achieves this aim; and if it does, it does so, I would suggest, because of an element in the play which in all the thousands of words I have read *about* the play, is rarely mentioned, i.e. the story.

I love stories. I spend all my writing life trying to make stories. The story, the narrative, which is unfashionable in the study of English

rationale [ˌræʃəˈnɑːl] explanation of reasons or principles **to masquerade as** [ˌmɑːskəˈreɪd] to pretend to be **relics** s.th. left from a past time **impenetrable** [ɪmˈpenɪtrəbl] impossible to understand **to engage s.o.** to compel the attention of s.o. **to be valid for** to be relevant to

literature, is to me all-important. A story, like a song, can transcend barriers of language, class and race. Sophisticates are suspicious of stories, believing that stories are only for children or the simple-minded. But a story is a difficult thing to make. It is a primal and magic thing and cannot be made by those who've turned their backs on simplicity.

During a radio interview a very respected and learned critic put it to me that the final moment of *Educating Rita* (where Rita cuts Frank's hair) was an allusion to Samson. The critic suggested that with the cutting of his hair Frank is losing his power as did Samson in a similar situation. I explained that, indeed, this was most definitely not the case, that I had merely chosen to end the play with a comic moment, a joke, a gag. Although I was the author of the play the critic argued with me, refused to accept my explanation (this part of the interview was edited from the final broadcast). The critic, the man of letters, could not accept the ignobility of my answer. He wanted my play to be less easily explained, less easily understood, wanted mystique. Amongst those who pass judgement on writing there is an awful belief that something which is easily understood and communicated is somehow inferior to that which requires profound analysis and explanation. It's rather like the situation in *Educating Rita* when Rita tells of seeing a marvellous coloured bird but is prevented from pointing it out to her teacher because, as the kids know, the teacher will not see the bird and its blazing colour but will see instead a subject for an essay.

I hope that you will find *Educating Rita* understandable without lengthy analysis and hope that, unlike the critic above, you will not think me lowbrow, unsound or inferior when I tell you that when making *Educating Rita* I tried very hard to write a love story. I hope I did.

Willy Russell. September 1983

to transcend to overcome **sophisticate** man of taste **primal** [ˈpraɪml] base, primitive; G. urmenschlich **to respect s.o.** to think highly of s.o. **to put s.th. to s.o.** to suggest s.th. to s.o. **allusion** an indirect reference; *G.* Anspielung **to edit** to alter (matter for publication) so as to make it more suitable for one's purpose; *here:* in the sense of to omit or leave out **ignobility** *G.* Niedrigkeit **inferior to** of poorer quality than **profound** *figurative:* deep **marvellous** very fine **kid** • child **blazing** bright **lowbrow** not intellectual; unscholarly **unsound** not based on well-grounded principles

EDUCATING RITA

First produced at The Warehouse, London, by the Royal Shakespeare Company, June 10th, 1980, and subsequently at the Piccadilly Theatre with the following cast of characters:

Frank	Mark Kingston
Rita	Julie Walters

Directed by Mike Ockrent
Designed by Poppy Mitchell

The action takes place in a first-floor room in a university in the north of England

Time – the present

ACT I

Scene 1

A room on the first floor of a Victorian-built university in the north of England
There is a large bay window L *with a desk placed in front of it and another desk* C *covered with various papers and books. The walls are lined with books and on one wall hangs a good print of a nude religious scene*
When the CURTAIN *rises Frank, who is in his early fifties, is standing* DRC *holding an empty mug. He goes to the bookcases* UR *and starts taking books from the shelves, hurriedly replacing them before moving on to another section*

Frank *(looking along the shelves)* Where the hell ...? Eliot? *(He pulls out some books and looks into the bookshelf).* No. *(He replaces the books)* "E". *(He thinks for a moment)* "E", "e" "e" ... *(Suddenly he remembers)* Dickens. *(Jubilantly he moves to the Dickens section and pulls out a pile of books to reveal a bottle of whisky. He*

Victorian built during the reign of Queen Victoria (1837–1901) **bay window** *G.* Erkerfenster **print** *here:* copy **mug** large cup without a saucer **Eliot** T.S. Eliot, Thomas Stearns Eliot (1888–1965), a major figure in English literature, poet and critic **Dickens** Charles Dickens (1812–1870), a famous English novelist **to reveal** to show

takes the bottle from the shelf and goes to the small table by the door and pours himself a large slug into the mug in his hand)

The telephone rings and startles him slightly. He manages a gulp at the whisky before he picks up the receiver and although his speech is not slurred, we should recognize the voice of a man who shifts a lot of booze

Yes? ... Of course I'm still here. ... Because I've got this Open University woman coming, haven't I? ... Tch. ... Of course I told you. ... But darling, you shouldn't have prepared dinner should you? Because I said, I distinctly remember saying that I would be late. ... Yes. Yes, I probably shall go to the pub afterwards, I shall need to go to the pub afterwards, I shall need to wash away the memory of some silly woman's attempts to get into the mind of Henry James or whoever it is we're supposed to study on this course. ... Oh God, why did I take this on? ... Yes. ... Yes I suppose I did take it on to pay for the drink. ... Oh, for God's sake, what is it? ... Yes, well – erm – leave it in the oven. ... Look if you're trying to induce some feeling of guilt in me over the prospect of a burnt dinner you should have prepared something other than lamb and ratatouille. ... Because, darling, I like my lamb done to the point of abuse and even I know that ratatouille cannot be burned. ... Darling, you could incinerate ratatouille and still it wouldn't burn. ... What do you mean am I determined to go to the pub? I don't need determination to get me into a pub ...

There is a knock at the door

Look, I'll have to go. ... There's someone at the door. ... Yes, yes I promise. ... Just a couple of pints. ... Four. ...

There is another knock at the door

(Calling in the direction of the door) Come in! *(He continues on the telephone)* Yes. ... All right ... yes. ... Bye, bye. ... *(He replaces*

slug• *G.* der Schluck; der Zug **he manages a gulp at the whisky** he only has time to quickly gulp down a small amount of whisky **slurred** indistinct; not spoken clearly **a man who shifts a lot of booze •** [bu:z] a man who drinks a lot of alcohol **to shift •** to move; *here:* to drink **booze •** alcohol **Open University** a non-residential university with its administrative centre in Milton Keynes, Buckinghamshire. It offers correspondence courses backed up by television and radio programmes, as well as summer schools and personal tuition. No previous formal academic qualifications are required for entry to its courses. **Henry James** (1843–1916), a major American novelist, playwright and storyteller **to induce** to produce **prospect** [ˈprɔspekt] *here:* idea **done** cooked **to the point of abuse** [əˈbju:s] for too long **to abuse** [əˈbju:z] to treat badly **to incinerate** [ɪnˈsɪnəreɪt] to set fire to **pint** [paɪnt] measure of beer (circa 0.57 of a litre)

the receiver) Yes, that's it, you just pop off and put your head in the oven. *(Shouting)* Come in! Come in!

The door swings open revealing Rita

Rita *(from the doorway)* I'm comin' in, aren't I? It's that stupid bleedin' handle on the door. You wanna get it fixed! *(She comes into the room)*

Frank *(staring, slightly confused)* Erm – yes, I suppose I always mean to ...

Rita *(going to the chair by the desk and dumping her bag)* Well that's no good, always meanin' to, is it? Y' should get on with it; one of these days you'll be shoutin' "Come in" an' it'll go on forever because the poor sod on the other side won't be *able* to get in. An' you won't be able to get out.

Frank stares at Rita who stands by the desk

Frank You are?

Rita What am I?

Frank Pardon?

Rita What?

Frank *(looking for the admission papers)* Now you are?

Rita I'm a what?

Frank looks up and then returns to the papers as Rita goes to hang her coat on the door hooks

(Noticing the picture) That's a nice picture, isn't it? *(She goes up to it)*

Frank Erm – yes, I suppose it is – nice ...

Rita *(studying the picture)* It's very erotic.

Frank *(looking up)* Actually I don't think I've looked at it for about ten years, but yes, I suppose it is.

Rita There's no suppose about it. Look at those tits.

He coughs and goes back to looking for the admission paper

Is it supposed to be erotic? I mean when he painted it do y' think he wanted to turn people on?

Frank Erm – probably.

Rita I'll bet he did y' know. Y' don't paint pictures like that just so that people can admire the brush strokes, do y'?

Frank *(giving a short laugh)* No – no – you're probably right.

to pop off • to go away quickly **bleedin'** ▲ *G.* verflucht **wanna** • want to; ought to **to dump** to put down carelessly **sod** ▲ person **admission paper** entrance form **to turn s.o. on** • to give s.o. pleasure or excitement **I'll bet he did** I'm certain he did **to bet** to risk your money on s.th. of which the result is doubtful

wetten

Rita This was the pornography of its day, wasn't it? It's sort of like *Men Only*, isn't it? But in those days they had to pretend it wasn't erotic so they made it religious, didn't they? Do *you* think it's erotic?

Frank *(taking a look)* I think it's very beautiful.

Rita I didn't ask y' if it was beautiful.

Frank But the term "beautiful" covers the many feelings I have about that picture, including the feeling that, yes, it is erotic.

Rita *(coming back to the desk)* D' y' get a lot like me?

Frank Pardon?

Rita Do you get a lot of students like me?

Frank Not exactly, no ...

Rita I was dead surprised when they took me. I don't suppose they would have done if it'd been a proper university. The Open University's different though, isn't it?

Frank I've – erm – not had much more experience of it than you. This is the first O.U. work I've done.

Rita D' y' need the money?

Frank I do as a matter of fact.

Rita It's terrible these days, the money, isn't it? With the inflation an' that. You work for the ordinary university, don't y'? With the real students. The Open University's different, isn't it?

Frank It's supposed to embrace a more comprehensive studentship, yes.

Rita *(inspecting a bookcase)* Degrees for dishwashers.

Frank Would you – erm – would you like to sit down?

Rita No! Can I smoke? *(She goes to her bag and rummages in it)*

Frank Tobacco?

Rita Yeh. *(She half-laughs)* Was that a joke? *(She takes out a packet of cigarettes and a lighter)* Here – d' y' want one? *(She takes out two cigarettes and dumps the packet on the desk)*

Frank *(after a pause)* Ah – I'd love one.

Rita Well, have one.

Frank *(after a pause)* I – don't smoke – I made a promise not to smoke.

Rita Well, I won't tell anyone.

• **Men Only** a sex magazine **term** expression **dead surprised** • extremely surprised **dead** • *here:* extremely, absolutely **to take s.o.** • to accept s.o. **proper** real; conventional **to embrace** *here:* to include **to rummage** [ˈrʌmɪdʒ] to search about **lighter** cigarette lighter

Frank Promise?

As Frank goes to take the cigarette Rita whips it from his reach

Rita *(doing a Brownie salute)* On my oath as an ex Brownie. *(She gives him the cigarette)* I hate smokin' on me own. An' everyone seems to have packed up these days. *(She lights the cigarettes)* They're all afraid of gettin' cancer.

Frank looks dubiously at his cigarette

But they're all cowards.

Frank Are they?

Rita You've got to challenge death an' disease. I read this poem about fightin' death ...

Frank Ah – Dylan Thomas ...

Rita No. Roger McGough. It was about this old man who runs away from hospital an' goes out on the ale. He gets pissed an' stands in the street shoutin' an' challengin' death to come out an' fight. It's dead good.

Frank Yes. I don't think I know the actual piece you mean ...

Rita I'll bring y' the book – it's great.

Frank Thank you.

Rita You probably won't think it's any good.

Frank Why?

Rita It's the sort of poetry you can understand.

Frank Ah. I see.

Rita begins looking idly round the room

Can I offer you a drink?

Rita What of?

Frank Scotch?

Rita *(going to the bookcase* UR*)* Y' wanna be careful with that stuff, it kills y' brain cells.

Frank But you'll have one? *(He gets up and goes to the small table)*

Rita All right. It'll probably have a job findin' my brain.

Frank *(pouring the drinks)* Water?

Rita *(looking at the bookcase)* Yeh, all right. *(She takes a copy of "Howards End" from the shelf)* What's this like?

Brownie junior member (aged 8–11) of the Girl Guides; *G.* Pfadfinder(in) **to pack (s.th.) up** • to stop **dubious** doubtful **to challenge** *G.* herausfordern **Dylan Thomas** Welsh poet (1914–1953) **Roger McGough** contemporary Liverpool poet and former member of "The Scaffold" pop group **to go out on the ale** to go out to drink (a lot) of beer **to get pissed** ▲ to get very drunk **actual** exact **idle** aimless **to have a job** • to have difficulty ***Howards End*** novel by E.M. Forster (1910)

Frank goes over to Rita, looks at the title of the book and then goes back to the drinks

Frank *Howards End*?

Rita Yeh. It sounds filthy, doesn't it? E.M. Foster.

Frank Forster.

Rita Oh yeh. What's it like?

Frank Borrow it. Read it.

Rita Ta. I'll look after it. *(She moves back towards the desk)* If I pack the course in I'll post it to y'.

Frank comes to the desk with the drinks

Frank *(handing her the mug)* Pack it in? Why should you do that?

Rita puts her drink down on the desk and puts the copy of "Howards End" in her bag

Rita I just might. I might decide it was a soft idea.

Frank *(looking at her)* Mm. Cheers. If – erm – if you're already contemplating "packing it in", why did you enrol in the first place?

Rita Because I wanna know.

Frank What do you want to know?

Rita Everything.

Frank Everything? That's rather a lot, isn't it? Where would you like to start?

Rita Well, I'm a student now, aren't? I'll have to do exams, won't I?

Frank Yes. Eventually.

Rita I'll have to learn about it all, won' I? Yeh. It's like y' sit there, don't y', watchin' the ballet or the opera on the telly an' – an' y' call it rubbish cos that's what it looks like? Cos y' don't understand. So y' switch it off an' say, that's fuckin' rubbish.

Frank Do you?

Rita I do. But I don't want to. I wanna see. Y' don't mind me swearin', do y'?

Frank Not at all.

Rita Do you swear?

Frank Never stop.

Rita See, the educated classes know it's only words, don't they? It's only the masses who don't understand. I do it to shock them sometimes. Y' know when I'm in the hairdresser's – that's where I

end rear; someone's rear is the part of the body they sit on **filthy** indecent **E.M. Forster** novelist and religious sceptic (1879–1970) **ta** • thank you **to look after s.th.** to take good care of s.th. **to pack s.th. in** • to give up s.th. **soft** • silly; stupid **Cheers** *G.* Prost **to enrol** to register; to sign on **exams** examinations **eventually** in the end **telly** • television **cos** • because **fuckin' rubbish** ▲ absolutely worthless **me** • my

work – I'll say somethin' like, "Oh, I'm really fucked", y' know, dead loud. It doesn't half cause a fuss.

Frank Yes – I'm sure ...

Rita But it doesn't cause any sort of fuss with educated people, does it? Cos they know it's only words and they don't worry. But these stuck-up idiots I meet, they think they're royalty just cos they don't swear; an' I wouldn't mind but it's the aristocracy that swears more than anyone, isn't? They're effin' an' blindin' all day long. It's all "Pass me the fackin' grouse" with them, isn't it? But y' can't tell them that round our way. It's not their fault; they can't help it. *(She goes to the window and looks out)* But sometimes I hate them. God, what's it like to be free?

Frank Ah. Now there's a question. Will you have another drink? *(He goes to the small table)*

Rita *(shaking her head)* If I'd got some other tutor I wouldn't have stayed.

Frank *(pouring himself a drink)* What sort of other tutor?

Rita Y' know, someone who objected to swearin'.

Frank How did you know I wouldn't object?

Rita I didn't. I was just testin' y'.

Frank *(coming back to the desk and looking at her)* Yes. You're doing rather a lot of that, aren't you?

Rita That's what I do. Y' know, when I'm nervous.

Frank *(sitting in the swivel chair)* And how am I scoring so far?

Rita Very good, ten out of ten go to the top of the class an' collect a gold star. I love this room. I love that window. Do you like it?

Frank What?

Rita The window.

Frank I don't often consider it actually. I sometimes get an urge to throw something through it.

Rita What?

Frank A student usually.

Rita *(smiling)* You're bleedin' mad you, aren't y'?

I'm really fucked ▲ I'm exhausted **it doesn't half** • it really does **fuss** excessive commotion, an outcry **stuck-up** • snobbish **effin' an' blindin'** ▲ swearing **fackin'** ▲ *G. etwa:* verflucht. (Vulgar expression used to show annoyance but often meaningless) **grouse** *G.* Moorhuhn. (Traditionally upper-class meal) **round our way** • in our neighbourhood **to object to s.th.** [əbˈdʒekt] to be against s.th. **swivel chair** [ˈswɪvl] a chair which turns on a pivot; *G.* Drehstuhl **to score** to gain points, goals etc. **How am I scoring?** How many points have I got? **ten out of ten** top marks; the best marks possible **gold star** (reference to the paper gold stars put on a good piece of work done by infant and junior school children) **urge** strong impulse

Frank Probably.

Pause

Rita Aren't you supposed to be interviewin' me?

Frank *(looking at the drink)* Do I need to?

Rita I talk too much, don't I? I know I talk a lot. I don't at home. I hardly ever talk when I'm there. But I don't often get the chance to talk to someone like you; to talk at you. D' y' mind?

Frank Would you be at all bothered if I did?

She shakes her head and then turns it into a nod

I don't mind. *(He takes a sip of his drink)*

Rita What does assonance mean?

Frank *(half-spluttering)* What? *(He gives a short laugh)*

Rita Don't laugh at me.

Frank No. Erm – assonance. Well, it's a form of rhyme. What's a – What's an example – erm –? Do you know Yeats?

Rita The wine lodge?

Frank Yeats the poet.

Rita No.

Frank Oh. Well – there's a Yeats poem, called *The Wild Swans at Coole*. In it he rhymes the word "swan" with the word "stone". There, you see, an example of assonance.

Rita Oh. It means gettin' the rhyme wrong.

Frank *(looking at her and laughing)* I've never really looked at it like that. But yes, yes you could say it means getting the rhyme wrong; but purposefully, in order to achieve a certain effect.

Rita Oh. *(There is a pause and she wanders round)* There's loads I don't know.

Frank And you want to know everything?

Rita Yeh.

Frank nods and then takes her admission paper from his desk and looks at it

Frank What's your name?

chance opportunity **to talk to s.o.** to speak to s.o.; to discuss s.th. with s.o. **to talk at s.o.** to speak to s.o. without listening to the replies **d' y' mind?** • do you mind?; do you object? **to be bothered** to be worried **to nod** *G.* nicken **sip** a small mouthful **assonance** ['æsənəns] agreement between stressed vowels in two words, but not in the following consonants, *e.g. sharper* and *garter* **half-spluttering** half swallowing, half spitting **Yeats** William Butler Yeats (1865–1939), major Irish poet **lodge** *here:* shop **wine lodge** *here:* Yates Wine Lodge (in the early eighties) a chain of wine bars in the north of England specializing in cheap Australian white wine; *cf.* "suffering from the whites", "too much wine in Yates". Nowadays they are to be found all over England and their image is much improved **to achieve** to produce **loads** • a lot **admission** registration

Rita *(moving towards the bookcase)* Rita.
Frank *(looking at the paper)* Rita. Mm. It says here Mrs S. White.
Rita goes to the right of Frank, takes a pencil, leans over and scratches out the initial "S"
Rita That's "S" for Susan. It's just me real name. I've changed it to Rita, though. I'm not a Susan anymore. I've called meself Rita – y' know, after Rita Mae Brown.
Frank Who?
Rita Y' know, Rita Mae Brown who wrote *Rubyfruit Jungle*? Haven't y' read it? It's a fantastic book. D' y' wanna lend it?
Frank I'd – erm – I'd be very interested.
Rita All right.
Rita gets a copy of "Rubyfruit Jungle" from her bag and gives it to Frank. He turns it over and reads the blurb on the back cover
What's your name?
Frank Frank.
Rita Oh. Not after Frank Harris?
Frank Not after Frank anyone.
Rita Maybe y' parents named y' after the quality. *(She sits in the chair by the desk)*
Frank puts down "Rubyfruit Jungle"
Y' know Frank, Frank Ness. Elliot's brother.
Frank What?
Rita I'm sorry – it was a joke. Y' know, Frank Ness, Elliot's brother.
Frank *(bemused)* Ah.
Rita You've still not got it, have y'? Elliot Ness – y' know, the famous Chicago copper who caught Al Capone.
Frank Ah. When you said Elliot I assumed you meant T.S. Eliot.
Rita Have you read his stuff?
Frank Yes.
Rita All of it?
Frank Every last syllable.

to scratch s.th. out to draw a line through **meseself** • myself **Rita Mae Brown** one of the founder mothers of both the gay and the women's movements **Rubyfruit Jungle** a novel about a proud, gutsy young girl; a popular best seller, written by Rita Mae Brown (1973) **d' y' wanna lend it?** • do you want to borrow it? **blurb** description **Frank Harris** refers to the English author (1856–1931) who achieved a posthumous notoriety with the English publication of *My Life and Loves* **quality** • *here:* frankness; G. Offenheit, Unbefangenheit **to get s.th.** • to understand **copper** • policeman **stuff** • *here:* works

Rita *(impressed)* Honest? I couldn't even get through one poem. I tried to read this thing he wrote called *J. Arthur Prufrock*; I couldn't finish it.

Frank *J. Alfred.*

Rita What?

Frank I think you'll find it was *J. Alfred Prufrock,* Rita. J. Arthur is something else altogether.

Rita Oh yeh. I never thought of that. I've not half got a lot to learn, haven't I?

Frank *(looking at her paper)* You're a ladies' hairdresser?

Rita Yeh.

Frank Are you good at it?

Rita *(getting up and wandering around)* I am when I wanna be. Most of the time I don't want to though. They get on me nerves.

Frank Who?

Rita The women. They never tell y' things that matter. Like, y' know, doin' a perm, well y' can't use a strong perm lotion on a head that's been bleached with certain sorts of cheap bleach. It makes all the hair break off. But at least once a month I'll get a customer in for a perm who'll swear to God that she's not had any bleach on; an' I can tell, I mean I can see it. So y' go ahead an' do the perm an' she comes out the drier with half an inch of stubble.

Frank And what do you do about it?

Rita Try and sell them a wig.

Frank My God.

Rita Women who want their hair doin', they won't stop at anythin', y' know. Even the pensioners are like that, y' know; a pensioner'll come in an' she won't tell y' that she's got a hearin' aid: so y' start cuttin' don't y'? Next thing – snip – another granny deaf for a fortnight. I'm always cuttin' hearin' aid cords. An' ear lobes.

Frank You sound like something of a liability.

honest • honestly, really **J. Alfred Prufrock** character in a poem by T.S. Eliot: *The Love Song of J. Alfred Prufrock.* **J. Arthur Rank** (1888–1972) founder of an entertainment company, the Rank Organisation, which owns and runs many film studios and cinemas **I've not half got a lot to learn** • I really do have a lot to learn **yeh** • yes **things that matter** important things **perm** *short form of:* permanent wave; *G.* Dauerwelle **to bleach** to make lighter in colour **drier** hair drier **stubble** *G.* Stoppel **wig** false hair **pensioners** senior citizens over 60 who receive a regular old age payment **hearin' aid** hearing aid; electronic instrument which helps deaf people to hear better **to snip** to make a short, quick cut **granny** *short form of:* grandmother **cord** *G.* Schnur **ear lobe** *G.* Ohrläppchen **liability** *here:* dangerous disadvantage, handicap

Rita I am. But they expect too much. They walk in the hairdresser's an' an hour later they wanna walk out a different person. I tell them I'm a hairdresser, not a plastic surgeon. It's worse when there's a fad on, y' know like Farrah Fawcett Majors.

Frank Who?

Rita Far-rah Fawcett Majors. Y' know, she used to be with *Charlie's Angels.*

Frank remains blank

It's a telly programme on ITV.

Frank Ah.

Rita *(wandering towards the door)* You wouldn't watch ITV though, would y'? It's all BBC with you, isn't it?

Frank Well, I must confess ...

Rita It's all right, I know. Soon as I walked in here I said to meself, "Y' can tell he's a *Flora* man".

Frank A what?

Rita A *Flora* man.

Frank Flora? Flowers?

Rita *(coming back to the desk)* No, *Flora*, the bleedin' margarine, no cholesterol; it's for people like you who eat pebble-dashed bread, y' know the bread, with little hard bits in it, just like pebble-dashin'.

Frank *(realizing and smiling)* Ah – pebble-dashed bread.

Rita Quick? He's like lightenin'. But these women, you see, they come to the hairdresser's cos they wanna be changed. But if you want to change y' have to do it from the inside, don't y'? Know like I'm doin'. Do y' think I'll be able to do it?

Frank Well, it really depends on you, on how committed you are. Are you sure that you're absolutely serious about wanting to learn?

there's a fad on • a particular thing is fashionable at the moment **Farrah Fawcett Majors** American actress ***Charlie's Angels*** American television detective series; G. *Drei Engel für Charlie* **blank** not understanding **I.T.V.** Independent Television – a television channel with advertising **B.B.C.** British Broadcasting Corporation – a television channel without advertising, thought by some to be more intellectual than I.T.V. **a Flora man** the advertising campaign for Flora margarine was one of the first (for a food product) aimed at men rather than women. The "Flora man" was portrayed as being the sensitive, health conscious, married man in his forties who helps his wife with the housework and children **pebble** very small, round stone; *G.* Kieselstein **pebble-dashed bread** (Rita's own expression) stone-ground (whole wheat) bread *G. etwa:* Dreikornbrot. (Usually white bread is eaten in England. Bioproducts are fashionable amongst the middle class.) **lightenin'** lightning *G.* (wie der) Blitz **know •** you know **committed** determined

Rita I'm dead serious. Look, I know I take the piss an' that but I'm dead serious really. I take the piss because I'm not, y' know, confident like, but I wanna be, honest.

He nods and looks at her. She becomes uncomfortable and moves away a little

Tch. What y' lookin' at me for?

Frank Because – I think you're marvellous. Do you know, I think you're the first breath of air that's been in this room for years.

Rita *(wandering around)* Tch. Now who's taking the piss?

Frank Don't you recognize a compliment?

Rita Go way ...

Frank Where to?

Rita Don't be soft. Y' know what I mean.

Frank What I want to know is what is it that's suddenly led you to this?

Rita What? Comin' here?

Frank Yes.

Rita It's not sudden.

Frank Ah.

Rita I've been realizin' for ages that I was, y' know, slightly out of step. I'm twenty-six. I should have had a baby by now; everyone expects it. I'm sure me husband thinks I'm sterile. He was moanin' all the time, y' know, "Come off the pill, let's have a baby". I told him I'd come off it, just to shut him up. But I'm still on it. *(She moves round to Frank)* See, I don't wanna baby yet. See, I wanna discover meself first. Do you understand that?

Frank Yes.

Rita *(moving to the chair* U *of the desk and fiddling with it)* Yeh. They wouldn't round our way. They'd think I was mental. I've tried to explain it to me husband but between you an' me I think he's thick. No, he's not thick, he's blind, he doesn't want to see. You know if I'm readin', or watchin' somethin' different on the telly he gets dead narked. I used to just tell him to piss off but then I realized that it was no good doin' that, that I had to explain to him. I tried to explain that I wanted a better way of livin' me life. An' he listened to me. But he didn't understand because when

I take the piss an' that ▲ I make fun of things **go way** • *here:* I can't believe that **soft** • silly **to be out of step** not to conform to the expectation of others **to moan** to complain **to come off s.th.** to stop taking **to be on s.th.** to take (medicine) **to fiddle** to play aimlessly **mental** • mad; crazy **thick** • stupid **dead narked** • very angry **to piss off** ▲ to go away

I'd finished he said he agreed with me and that we should start savin' the money to move off our estate an' get a house out in Formby. Even if it was a new house I wanted I wouldn't go an' live in Formby. I hate that hole, don't you?

Frank Yes.

Rita Where do you live?

Frank Formby.

Rita *(sitting)* Oh.

Frank *(getting up and going to the small table)* Another drink?

She shakes her head

You don't mind if I do? *(He pours himself a drink)*

Rita No. It's your brain cells y' killin'.

Frank *(smiling)* All dead long ago I'm afraid. *(He drinks)*

Rita gets up and goes to Frank's chair. She plays with the swivel and then leans on it

Rita When d' y' actually, y' know, start teaching me?

Frank *(looking at her)* What can I teach you?

Rita Everything.

Frank leans on the filing cabinet, drinks, shakes his head and looks at her

Frank I'll make a bargain with you. Yes? I'll tell you everything I know – but if I do that you must promise never to come back here ... You see I never – I didn't actually want to take this course in the first place. I allowed myself to be talked into it. I knew it was wrong. Seeing you only confirms my suspicion. My dear, it's not your fault, just the luck of the draw that you got me; but get me you did. And the thing is, between you, me and the walls, I'm actually an appalling teacher. *(After a pause)* Most of the time, you see, it doesn't actually matter – appalling teaching is quite in order for most of my appalling students. And the others manage to get by despite me. But you're different. You want a lot, and I can't give it. *(He moves towards her)* Everything I know – and you must listen to this – is that I know absolutely nothing. I don't like the hours, you know. *(He goes to the swivel chair and sits)* Strange hours for this Open University thing. They expect us to teach when the pubs are open. I can be a good teacher when I'm in the

estate housing estate; area of houses usually belonging to the Local Government Housing Department **Formby** residential suburb of Liverpool **filing cabinet** document cupboard **to make a bargain** to come to an agreement **suspicion** G. Verdacht **it's not your fault** you are not to blame **the draw** the lottery **appalling** [ə'pɔ:lɪŋ] extremely bad **actually** really **to get by** to survive; to succeed

pub, you know. Four pints of weak *Guinness* and I can be as witty as Wilde. I'm sorry – there are other tutors – I'll arrange it for you ... post it on ... *(He looks at her)*

Rita slowly turns and goes towards the door. She goes out and quietly closes the door behind her. Suddenly the door bursts open and Rita flies in

Rita *(going up to him)* Wait a minute, listen to me. Listen: I'm on this course, your are my teacher – an' you're gonna bleedin' well teach me.

Frank There are other tutors – I've told you ...

Rita You're my tutor. I don't want another tutor.

Frank For God's sake, woman – I've told you ...

Rita You're my tutor.

Frank But I've told you – I don't want to do it. Why come to me?

Rita *(looking at him)* Because you're a crazy mad piss artist who wants to throw his students through the window, an' I like you. *(After a pause)* Don't you recognize a compliment?

Frank Do you think I could have a cigarette?

Rita *(offering the packet of cigarettes)* I'll bring me scissors next week and give y' a haircut.

Frank You're not coming here next week.

Rita *(lighting his cigarette)* I am. And you're gettin' y' hair cut.

Frank I am not getting my hair cut.

Rita *(getting her bag)* I suppose y' wanna walk round like that, do y'? *(She goes towards the door)*

Frank Like what?

Rita *(getting her coat)* Like a geriatric hippie.

Black-out

Rita exits

Guinness a type of Irish stout (a very dark bitter beer) – traditionally a working-class drink **Wilde** Oscar Wilde (1854–1900), well-known dramatist and poet **you're gonna bleedin' well teach me** ▲ you are going to teach me whether you want to or not **piss artist** ▲ s.o. who is often drunk **to get s.th. done** to have s.th. done **geriatric hippie** [ˌdʒerɪˈætrɪk] very old hippie **geriatrics** medical care of old people

Scene 2

The Lights come up on Frank who is standing in the centre of the room. He glances at his watch, moves to the window, looks out, glances at his watch again and then moves across to the books. He glances at his watch and then his attention is caught by the door handle being turned. He looks at the door but no-one enters although the handle keeps being turned. Eventually he goes to the door and pulls it open Rita is standing in the doorway, holding a small can of oil

Frank Oh.

Rita Hello. I was just oilin' it for y'. *(She comes into the room)* I knew you wouldn't get round to it. Y' can have that.

She gives the oil can to Frank

Frank Erm – thanks. *(He puts the can on the filing cabinet and then goes and sits in the swivel chair)*

Slightly amused, he watches her as she wanders round the room

Rita *(turning to him)* What y' lookin' at?

Frank Don't you ever just walk into a room and sit down?

Rita Not when I've got the chair with its back to the door.

Frank *(getting up)* Well – if it'd make you happier you take my chair.

Rita No. You're the teacher, you sit there.

Frank But it doesn't matter where I sit. If you'd be happier with that chair then you sit there.

Rita Tch. Is that what y' call democracy at work? I don't wanna sit down anyway. I like walkin' around this room. *(After a pause)* How d' y' make a room like this?

Frank I didn't make it. I just moved in. The rest sort of happened.

Rita *(looking round)* Yeh. That's cos you've got taste. I'm gonna have a room like this one day. There's nothing phoney about it. Everything's in its right place. *(After a pause)* It's a mess. But it's a perfect mess. *(She wanders around)* It's like wherever you've put something down it's grown to fit there.

Frank *(sitting down)* You mean that over the years it's acquired a certain patina.

to glance at to take a quick look at **to get round to s.th.** to do s.th. only after dealing with more important matters **sort of** somehow **phoney** not genuine **mess** state of confusion or disorder **to fit to** look right or suitable **to acquire** to gain; to get **patina** ['pætɪnə] green glossy surface formed on copper

Rita Do I?

Frank I think so.

Rita Yeh. "It's acquired a certain patina." It's like somethin' from a romantic film, isn't it? "Over the years your face has acquired a certain patina." sicher/zuverlässige

Frank smiles

(Sniffing) You've not been drinking, have y'?

Frank No.

Rita Is that because of me, because of what I said last week?

Frank *(laughing)* My God. You think you've reformed me?

Rita *(going to the window)* I don't wanna reform y'. Y' can do what y' like. *(Quickly)* I love that lawn down there. When it's summer do they sit on it?

Frank *(going to the window)* Who?

Rita *(going back to the desk)* The ones who come here all the time. The proper students.

Frank Yes. First glimmer of sun and they're all out there.

Rita Readin' an' studyin'?

Frank Reading and studying? What do you think they are, human? Proper students don't read and study.

Rita Y' what?

Frank A joke, a joke. Yes. They read and study, sometimes.

Pause. Rita dumps her bag on the chair and then goes and hangs up her coat on the door

Rita It looks the way I always imagined a public school to look, y' know a boardin' school. When I was a kid I always wanted to go to a boardin' school.

Frank God forbid it; why?

Rita *(going to her chair at the desk)* I always thought they sounded great, schools like that, y' know with a tuck-shop an' a matron an' prep. An' a pair of kids called Jones minor an' Jones major. I told me mother once. *(She opens her bag and takes out the copy of "Howards End", ring bound file, note-pad, ruler and pencil-case,*

to sniff *G.* schnuppern **lawn** smooth area of grass cut very short **proper (students)** real (university students) **Y' what?** I beg your pardon; *G.* Wie bitte? **public school** school for fee-paying pupils **boarding school** school where children live and take lessons **kid** • child **great** marvellous **tuck-shop** school shop which sells sweets and cakes **matron** woman housekeeper and nurse in a school **prep** time given at school to prepare lessons and do homework **Jones minor** the younger boy called Jones **Jones major** the older boy called Jones. (These are character types which often appear in children's stories about life in boarding schools.) **ring bound file** ring-binder; *G.* Ringbuch

placing them methodically on the desk in front of her) She said I was off me cake.

Frank *(with an exaggerated look at her)* What in the name of God is being off one's cake?

Rita Soft. Y' know, mental.

Frank Aha. I must remember that. The next student to ask me if Isabel Archer was guilty of protestant masochism shall be told that one is obviously very off one's cake!"

Rita Don't be soft. You can't say that.

Frank Whyever not?

Rita You can't. If you do it, it's slummin' it. Comin' from you it'd sound dead affected, wouldn't it?

Frank Dead affected?

Rita Yeh. You say that to your proper students they'll think you're off your – y' know ...

Frank Cake, yes. Erm – Rita, why didn't you ever become what you call a proper student?

Rita What? After goin' to the school I went to?

Frank Was it bad?

Rita starts sharpening the pencils one by one into perfect spikes, leaving the shavings on the desk

Rita Nah, just normal, y' know; borin', ripped-up books, broken glass everywhere, knives an' fights. An' that was just in the staffroom. Nah, they tried their best I suppose, always tellin' us we stood more of a chance if we studied. But studyin' was just for the whimps, wasn't it? See, if I'd started takin' school seriously I would have had to become different from me mates, an' that's not allowed.

Frank By whom?

Rita By your mates, by your family, by everyone. So y' never admit that school could be anythin' other than useless.

Frank passes her the ashtray but she ignores it and continues sharpening the pencils on to the table

Like what you've got to be into is music an' clothes an' lookin' for a feller, y' know the real qualities of life. Not that I went along

to be off one's cake • to be mad **to exaggerate** *G.* übertreiben **Isabel Archer** heroine of Henry James' novel *The Portrait of a Lady* **to slum it** • to behave and live in a way below your social position **dead** • very **affected** • not natural, done only to impress s.o. **spike** *here:* long sharp point **to rip up** *G.* zerreißen **staffroom** teacher's room **to stand a chance** to have a chance **whimps** ▲ weak, spineless characters **mate** • friend **to admit** to acknowledge **to be into s.th.** to be interested in s.th. **feller** • fellow; boyfriend **to go along with s.th.** to agree with s.th.; to accept s.th.

with it so reluctantly. I mean, there was always somethin' in me head, tappin' away, tellin' me I might have got it all wrong. But I'd just play another record or buy another dress an' stop worryin'. There's always somethin' to make you forget about it. So y' do, y' keep goin', tellin' yourself life's great. There's always another club to go to, a new feller to be chasin', a laugh an' a joke with the girls. Till, one day, y' own up to yourself an' y' say, is this it? Is this the absolute maximum I can expect from this livin' lark? An' that's the big moment that one, that's the point when y' have to decide whether it's gonna be another change of dress or a change in yourself. An' it's really temptin' to go out an' get another dress y' know, it is. Cos it's easy, it doesn't cost anythin', it doesn't upset anyone around y'. Like cos they don't want y' to change.

Frank But you – erm – you managed to resist another new dress?

Rita Can't y' tell? Look at the state of this; I haven't had a new dress in twelve months. An' I'm not gonna get one either, not till – till I pass me first exam. Then I'll get a proper dress, the sort of dress you'd only see on an educated woman, on the sort of woman who knows the difference between Jane Austen an' Tracy Austin. *(She finishes sharpening the last pencil, and arranges it in line with the others. She gathers the pencil shavings into her hand and chucks them in the waste-bin)* Let's start.

Frank Now the piece you wrote for me on – what was it called ...?

Rita *(getting out her cigarettes and lighter) Rubyfruit Jungle.*

Frank Yes, it was – erm ...

Rita Crap?

Frank No. Erm – the thing is, it was an appreciation, a descriptive piece. What you have to learn is criticism.

Rita What's the difference? *(She lights a cigarette)*

Frank Well. You must try to remember that criticism is purely objective. It should be approached almost as a science. It must be supported by reference to established literary critique. Criticism is never subjective and should not be confused with partisan interpretation. In criticism sentiment has no place. *(He picks up the*

reluctant [rɪ'lʌktənt] unwilling **to own up** to confess **lark** • *here:* game **temptin'** tempting; *G.* verführerisch **to upset s.o.** to trouble; to disturb s.o. **state** condition **Jane Austen** English novelist (1775–1817) **Tracy Austin** top American tennis star in the early eighties **to chuck** • to throw **crap** ▲ rubbish **appreciation** statement of one's own ideas **to approach** to handle **to support** to use facts to confirm s.th. **critique** [krɪ'ti:k] *here:* articles, books on criticism

copy of "Howards End") Tell me, what did you think of *Howards End*?

Rita It was crap.

Frank What?

Rita I thought it was crap!

Frank Crap? And who are you citing in support of your thesis, F.R. Leavis?

Rita No. Me!

Frank What have I just said? "Me" is subjective.

Rita Well it's what I think.

Frank You think *Howards End* is crap? Well would you kindly tell me why you think it's quote, "Crap", unquote.

Rita Yeh, I will tell y'. It's crap because the feller who wrote it was a louse. Because halfway through that book I couldn't go on readin' it because he, Mr Bleedin' E.M. Forster says, quote "We are not concerned with the poor" unquote. That's why it's crap. An' that's why I didn't go on readin' it, that's why.

Frank *(astounded)* Because he said we are not concerned with the poor?

Rita Yeh, that's it!

Frank But he wasn't writing about the poor.

Rita When he wrote that book the conditions of the poor in this country were appalling. An' he's sayin' he couldn't care less. Mr E.M. Bleedin' Foster.

Frank Forster.

Rita I don't care what his name was, he was sittin' up there in his ivory tower an' sayin' he couldn't care less.

Frank laughs

Don't laugh at me.

Frank *(getting up)* But you cannot interpret E.M. Forster from a Marxist viewpoint.

Rita Why?

Frank Look, before discussing this I said no subjectivity, no sentimentality.

Rita I wasn't bein' sentimental.

F.R. Leavis Frank Raymond Leavis (1895–1978), influential literary critic **louse** ▲ useless person **astounded** completely surprised or shocked **he couldn't care less** *G.* er macht sich nicht das Geringste daraus **ivory** *G.* Elfenbein **in his ivory tower** cut off from the realities of life

„in seinem eisernen Käfig"

Frank Of course you were. You stopped reading the book because you wanted Forster to concern himself with the poor. Literature can ignore the poor.

Rita Well, it's immoral.

Frank *(wandering around)* Amoral. But you wanted to know. You see what sort of a mark you'd get if you approached Forster in this way during an examination?

Rita What sort?

Frank Well, you might manage one or two per cent if the examiner was sympathetic to the one dubious quality your criticism displays.

Rita What's that?

Frank Brevity.

Rita All right. But I hated that book. Can't we do somethin' else? Can't we do somethin' I like?

Frank But the sort of stuff you like is not necessarily the sort of thing that will form the basis of your examination next Christmas. Now if you're going to pass any sort of exam you have to begin to discipline that mind of yours.

Rita Are you married?

Frank *(moving back to the swivel chair)* It's – ogh ...

Rita Are y'? What's y' wife like?

Frank Is my wife at all relevant?

Rita What? You should know, you married her.

Frank Well, she's not relevant. I haven't seen her for a long time. We split up. All right?

Rita I'm sorry.

Frank Why are you sorry?

Rita I'm sorry for askin'. For bein' nosey.

Frank *(sitting in the swivel chair)* The thing about *Howards End* is that ...

Rita Why did y' split up?

Frank *(taking off his glasses and looking at her)* Perhaps you'd like to take notes! When you have to answer a question on Forster you can treat the examiner to an essay called Frank's marriage!

Rita Oh go way. I'm only interested.

mark *G.* Note, Prädikat **sympathetic** *G.* wohlwollend **brevity** shortness **stuff** • thing(s) (used to suggest anything of inferior quality) **to split up** to get divorced **nosey** inquisitive; *G.* neugierig **to treat s.o. to s.th.** to give s.o. s.th. special as a friendly act; *G.* spendieren

Frank *(leaning towards her; conspiratorially)* We split up, Rita, because of poetry.

Rita Y' what?

Frank One day my wife pointed out to me that for fifteen years my output as a poet had dealt exclusively with the period in which we – discovered each other.

Rita Are you a poet?

Frank Was. And so, to give me something new to write about she left. A very noble woman my wife. She left me for the good of literature.

Rita An' what happened?

Frank She was right. Her leaving was an enormous benefit to literature.

Rita What, y' wrote a load of good stuff?

Frank No. I stopped writing altogether.

Rita *(slightly puzzled)* Are you takin' the piss?

Frank gives a short laugh and leans back in his chair

Frank No.

Rita People don't split up because of things like that. Because of literature.

Frank Maybe you're right. But that's how I remember it.

Rita Were you a famous poet?

Frank No. I sold a few books, all out of print now.

Rita Can I read some of your stuff?

Frank You wouldn't like it.

Rita How d' y' know?

Frank It's the sort of poetry you can't understand – unless you happen to have a detailed knowledge of the literary references.

Rita Oh. *(After a pause)* Do you live on y' own then?

Frank Rita! Tch.

Rita I was only askin'.

Frank I live with a girl. Ex student. She's very caring, very tolerant, admires me enormously and spends a great deal of time putting her head in the oven.

Rita Does she try an' do herself in?

to point s.th. out to draw s.o.'s attention to s.th. **output** result of work **to deal with s.th.** to be about s.th. **noble** fine **for the good of** for the benefit of; to help **a load of good stuff** • a lot of good material **puzzled** confused **to take the piss** ▲ *G.* verarschen **out of print** no longer being printed **to happen to have** to have by chance **to do oneself in** • to commit suicide

Frank Mm? No, she just likes to watch the ratatouille cook.

Rita The what?

Frank Ratatouille. Though Julia has renamed it the "stop-outs dish". It can simmer in an oven for days. In our house it often has no choice.

Rita D' you stop out for days?

Frank Occasionally. And that is the end of ... Gelegentlich.

Rita Why do y'?

Frank And that is the end of that.

Rita If y' were mine an' y' stopped out for days y' wouldn't get back in.

Frank Ah, but Rita, if I was yours would I stop out for days?

Rita Don't y' like Julia?

Frank I like her enormously; it's myself I'm not too fond of.

Rita Tch. Y' great ...

Frank A vote of confidence; thank you. But, I'm afraid, Rita, that you'll find there's less to me than meets the eye.

Rita See – look – y' can say dead clever things like that, can't y'? I wish I could talk like that. It's brilliant.

Frank Staggering. Now look, *Howards ... (He swivels the chair round so that he faces away from Rita)*

Rita Oh ey ... leave that. I just like talkin' to y'. It's great. That's what they do wrong in schools y' know – *(she gets up and warms her legs by the fire)* – they get y' talkin' an' that, an' y' all havin' a great time talkin' about somethin' an' the next thing they wanna do is turn it into a lesson. We was out with the teacher once, y' know outside school, an' I'm right at the back with these other kids an' I saw this fantastic bird, all coloured it was, like dead out of place round our way. I was just gonna shout an' tell Miss but this kid next to me said, "Keep your mouth shut or she'll make us write an essay on it."

Frank *(sighing)* Yes, that's what we do, Rita; we call it education.

Rita Tch. Y'd think there was somethin' wrong with education to hear you talk.

Frank Perhaps there is.

Rita So why are y' givin' me an education?

to simmer to cook slowly without boiling **if y' were mine** if you were my husband **to stop out** to stay away from home **vote of confidence** expression of support; *G.* Vertrauensvotum **there's less to me than meets the eye** *usual form:* there's more than meets the eye, *i.e.* to have hidden qualities **staggering** • astonishing **Miss** way of addressing a lady teacher

Frank Because it's what you want, isn't it? What I'd actually like to do is take you by the hand and run out of this room forever.

Rita *(going back to her chair)* Tch – be serious ...

Frank I am. Right now there's a thousand things I'd rather do than teach; most of them with you, young lady ...

Rita *(smiling gently)* Tch. Oh sod off ... You just like saying things like that. *(She sits down).*

Frank Do I?

Rita Yeh. Y' know y' do.

Frank Rita – why didn't you walk in here twenty years ago?

Rita Cos I don't think they would have accepted me at the age of six.

Frank You know what I mean.

Rita I know. But it's not twenty years ago, Frank. It's now. You're there an' I'm here.

Frank Yes. And you're here for an education. *(He waves his finger)* You must keep reminding me of that. Come on, Forster!

Rita Tch. Forget him.

Frank Listen to me; you said that I was going to teach you. You want to learn. Well that, I'm afraid, means a lot of work. You've barely had a basic schooling, you've never passed an examination in your life. Possessing a hungry mind is not, in itself, a guarantee of success.

Rita All right. But I just don't like *Howards* bleedin' *End.*

Frank Then go back to what you do like and stop wasting my time. You go out and buy yourself a new dress and I'll go to the pub.

Rita *(after a pause)* Is that you putting your foot down?

Frank It is actually.

Rita Oh. Aren't you impressive when y' angry?

Frank Forster!

Rita All right, all right, Forster. Does Forster's repeated use of the phrase "only connect" suggest that he was really a frustrated electrician?

Frank Rita.

Rita In considering Forster it helps if we examine the thirteen amp plug ...

Black-out

Rita goes out

sod off ▲ go away **barely** only just; hardly **schooling** education **to put one's foot down** to speak and act firmly **to connect** *G.* verbinden, kombinieren, elektrisch anschließen **amp** ampere **plug** *G.* Stecker

Scene 3

The Lights come up on Frank working at his desk
Rita flounces into the room and goes to the desk

Rita God, I've had enough of this. It's borin', that's what it is, bloody borin'. This Forster, honest to God he doesn't half get on my tits.

She dumps her bag on the chair and makes towards the hook by the door, taking off her coat as she goes. She hangs the coat on the hook

Frank Good. You must show me the evidence.

Rita Y' dirty sod.

Frank *(wagging his finger at her)* True, true ... it's cutting down on the booze that's done it. Now. *(He waves a sheet of paper at her)* What's this?

Rita *(sitting by the desk)* It's a bleedin' piece of paper, isn't it?

Frank It's your essay. Is it a joke? Is it?

Rita No. It's not a joke.

Frank Rita, how the hell can you write an essay on E.M. Forster with almost total reference to Harold Robbins?

Rita Well? You said bring in other authors.

Frank Tch.

Rita Don't go on at me. You said; y' said, "Reference to other authors will impress the examiners".

Frank I said refer to other works but I don't think the examiner, God bless him, will have read, *(he consults the paper) A Stone For Danny Fisher.*

Rita Well, that's his hard luck, isn't it?

Frank It'll be your hard luck when he fails your paper.

Rita Oh that's prime, isn't it? That's justice for y'. I get failed just cos I'm more well read than the friggin' examiner!

Frank Devouring pulp fiction is not being well read.

to flounce to move quickly and impatiently **he doesn't half get on my tits** ▲ he really does get on my nerves **evidence** proof **dirty sod** ▲ (vulgar term of abuse for a person) **booze** • alcoholic drink **Harold Robbins** popular American novelist (born 1916) ***A Stone For Danny Fisher*** a novel about a boxer who could have been one of the great ones; it is set in the city of New York **hard luck** bad luck **to fail s.th.** to decide a piece of work is not good enough to pass an examination **prime** • marvellous **friggin'** ▲ G. verflucht **to devour** [dɪ'vaʊə] to eat greedily or hungrily **pulp fiction** cheap, popular magazines and books **to be well read** to have a good background education gained from books

Rita I thought reading was supposed to be good for one. *(She gets out her cigarettes)*

Frank It is, but you've got to be selective. In your favour you do mention *Sons and Lovers* somewhere in here. When did you read that?

Rita This week. I read that an' the Harold Robbins an' this dead fantastic book, what was it called? Erm – ogh what was it? It sounded like somethin' dead perverted, it was by that English feller ...

Frank Which English feller?

Rita You know, the one who was like Noël Coward – erm. Oh, I know – Somerset Maugham.

Frank A perverted book by Somerset Maugham?

Rita No, it wasn't perverted it was great – the title sounds perverted ...

He starts to laugh

Don't laugh.

Frank Do you mean *Of Human Bondage*?

Rita Yeh – that's it. Well it does sound perverted doesn't it?

Frank Well! *(After a pause)* You read three novels this week?

Rita *(taking a cigarette from the pack).* Yeh. It was dead quiet in the shop.

Frank And if I asked you to make a comparison between those books, what would you say?

Rita Well, they were all good in their own way.

Frank But surely you can see the difference between the Harold Robbins and the other two.

Rita Apart from that one bein' American like?

Frank Yes.

Rita Yeh. I mean the other two were sort of posher. But they're all books, aren't they?

Frank Yes. Yes. But you seem to be under the impression that all books are literature.

Rita Aren't they?

Frank No.

Rita Well – well how d' y' tell?

Sons and Lovers novel by D.H. Lawrence (1913), British novelist, story-writer, poet and critic (1885–1930) **Noël Coward** (1899–1973), popular English actor, dramatist and composer **Somerset Maugham** (1874–1965), famous English novelist, story-writer, dramatist and critic **perverted** unnatural, abnormal ***Of Human Bondage*** novel by Somerset Maugham (1915) **bondage** *G.* Knechtschaft; also: being tied up in order to gain sexual pleasure **like** • you understand (an expression of hesitancy particular to northern speech) **posher** • [ˈpɑʃə] more intellectual **how d' y' tell ...?** • how do you tell ...?; how do you distinguish?

Frank I – erm – erm – one's always known really.

Rita But how d' y' work it out if y' don't know? See that's what I've got to learn, isn't it? I'm dead ignorant y' know.

Frank No. You're not ignorant. It's merely a question of becoming discerning in your choice of reading material.

Rita I've got no taste. Is that what you're saying?

Frank No.

Rita It is. Don't worry. I won't get upset. I'm here to learn. My mind's full of junk, isn' it? It needs a good clearin' out. Right, that's it, I'll never read a Robbins' novel again.

Frank Read it, by all means read it. But don't mention it in an exam.

Rita Aha. You mean, it's all right to go out an' have a bit of slap an' tickle with the lads as long as you don't go home an' tell your mum?

Frank Erm – well yes, that's probably what I do mean.

Black-out

Rita exits

Scene 4

The Lights come up on Frank who is standing by the window

Rita enters and shuts the door behind her, standing just inside the room

Frank goes to his briefcase on the window-desk and starts looking for Rita's "Peer Gynt" essay

Rita I can't do it. Honest, I just can't understand what he's on about. *(She goes to her chair at the desk, dumps her bag and then goes and hangs up her coat)* He's got me licked, I don't know what he's on about. "Only connect, only connect", it's just bleedin' borin'. It's no good, I just can't understand.

Frank You will. You will.

Rita It's all right for you sayin' that. You know what it's about. *(She goes to her chair by the desk)* But I just can't figure it.

to work s.th. out to find an answer; to come to a conclusion **merely** just; simply **to be discerning** to understand well and form opinions **upset** emotionally disturbed **junk** useless things **a clearin' out** when useless things are taken (out of a room) and thrown away **a bit of slap and tickle** a bit of fun **lads** young men; boys ***Peer Gynt*** play by Ibsen (1866). Henrik Ibsen (1828–1906) was a famous Norwegian dramatist **honest** • honestly **it's got me licked** it's too difficult for me, I cannot do it **to be on about s.th.** • to talk about s.th. **to figure s.th. (out)** • to work s.th. out; to understand

Frank Do you think we could forget about Forster for a moment?

Rita With pleasure.

Frank takes the "Peer Gynt" essay and stands over her for a moment. Then he perches on the corner of the desk UL

Frank I want to talk about this that you sent me. *(He holds up a sheet of A4 paper)*

Rita That? Oh.

Frank Yes. In response to the question, "Suggest how you would resolve the staging difficulties inherent in a production of Ibsen's *Peer Gynt*", you have written, quote, "Do it on the radio", unquote.

Rita Precisely.

Frank Well?

Rita Well what?

Frank Well I know it's probably quite naïve of me but I did think you might let me have a considered essay.

Rita sits down by the desk and unpacks the student's pad, pencil case, ruler, copy of "Peer Gynt" and eight reference books from her bag

Rita That's all I could do in the time. We were dead busy in the shop this week.

Frank You write your essays at work?

Rita Yeh.

Frank Why?

Rita Denny get's dead narked if I work at home. He doesn't like me doin' this. I can't be bothered arguin' with him.

Frank But you can't go on producing work as thin as this.

Rita Is it wrong?

Frank No, it's not wrong, it's just ...

Rita See, I know it's short. But I thought it was the right answer.

Frank It's the basis for an argument, Rita, but one line is hardly an essay.

Rita I know, but I didn't have much time this week, so I sort of, y' know, encapsulated all me ideas in one line.

Frank But it's not enough.

Rita Why not?

Frank It just isn't.

A4 paper *G.* DIN A 4-Bogen **to resolve** to find a solution to **staging** method of presenting a play on the stage of a theatre **inherent** existing as a natural part of s.th. **considered** carefully thought about **reference book** book used to look up information **dead narked** very annoyed **to encapsulate** to express in the fewest possible words

Rita But that's bleedin' stupid, cos you say – you say, don't y' – that one line of exquisite poetry says more than a thousand pages of second-rate prose?

Frank But you're not writing poetry. What I'm trying to make you see is that whoever was marking this would want more than, "Do it on the radio". *(He gets up and moves around to the other side of Rita's chair)* There is a way of answering examination questions that is expected. It's a sort of accepted ritual, it's a game, with rules. And you must observe those rules. *(He leans with one hand on the back of Rita's chair)* When I was at university there was a student taking his final theology exam. He walked into the examination hall, took out his pen and wrote "God knows all the answers", then he handed in his paper and left.

Rita *(impressed)* Did he?

Frank When his paper was returned to him, his professor had written on it, "And God gives out the marks".

Rita Did he fail?

Frank *(breaking away slightly)* Of course he failed. You see, a clever answer is not necessarily the correct answer.

Rita *(getting out her cigarettes)* I wasn't tryin' to be clever; I didn't have much time an' I ...

Frank All right, but look, you've got some time now. *(He leans on her chair, bending over her)* Just give it a quarter of an hour or so adding some considered argument to this: "In attempting to resolve the staging difficulties in *Peer Gynt* I would present it on the radio because ..." and outline your reasons supporting them, as much as possible, with quotes from accepted authorities. All right?

Rita Yeh. All right. *(She picks up the essay, pen, copy of "Peer Gynt", eight reference books, sticks the cigarette in her mouth, and starts to move towards the window desk)*

Frank Now, are you sure you understand?

Rita stops and speaks over her shoulder with the cigarette still in her mouth

Rita Yeh. What d' y' think I am, thick? *(She takes her usual chair and puts it in front of the window desk. She sits down and puts her belongings on the desk, moving Frank's briefcase out of the way)*

second-rate inferior quality **to mark** to correct **to fail** to be unsuccessful **accepted authority** person or book with specialized knowledge and reliable information **thick** stupid **briefcase** *G.* Aktentasche

Frank moves the swivel chair to the U *end of his desk and settles down to marking essays*
Rita leans back in the chair and tries to blow smoke-rings
Y' know Peer Gynt? He was searchin' for the meaning of life wasn't he?

Frank Erm – put at its briefest, yes.

Rita Yeh. *(She pauses)* I was doin' this woman's hair on Wednesday ...

Frank Tch ...

Rita *(facing Frank)* I'm gonna do this, don't worry. I'll do it. But I just wanna tell y'; I was doin' her hair an' I was dead bored with what the others in the shop were talkin' about. So I just said to this woman, I said, "Do you know about *Peer Gynt*?" She thought it was a new perm lotion. So I told her all about it, y' know the play. An' y' know somethin', she was dead interested, she was y' know.

Frank Was she?

Rita Yeh. She said, "I wish I could go off searchin' for the meanin' of life." There's loads of them round by us who feel like that. Cos by us there is no meanin' to life. *(She thinks)* Frank, y' know culture, y' know the word culture? Well it doesn't just mean goin' to the opera an' that, does it?

Frank No.

Rita It means a way of livin', doesn't it? Well we've got no culture.

Frank Of course you have.

Rita What? Do you mean like that working-class culture thing?

Frank Mm.

Rita Yeh. I've read about that. I've never seen it though.

Frank Well, look around you.

Rita I do. But I don't see any, y' know, culture. I just see everyone pissed, or on the *Valium*, tryin' to get from one day to the next. Y' daren't say that round our way like, cos they're proud. They'll tell y' they've got culture as they sit there drinkin' their keg beer out of plastic glasses.

Frank Yes, but there's nothing wrong with that, if they're content with it.

to settle down to to begin to give one's full attention to **round by us** • in our neighbourhood **pissed** ▲ drunk **Valium** a very addictive drug given to reduce stress and anxiety **like** • you know **keg** small barrel **keg beer** brown beer (similar to 'Altbier', but of much poorer quality) **content** [kən'tent] satisfied and happy

During the following Frank's attention is caught gradually and he stops marking and starts listening

Rita But they're not. Cos there's no meanin'. They tell y' stories about the past, y' know, the war, or when they were fightin' for food an' clothin' an' houses. Their eyes light up as they tell y', because there was some meanin' to it. But the thing is that now, I mean now that most of them have got some sort of house an' there's food an' money around, they know they're better off but, honest, they know they've got nothin' as well. There's like this sort of disease, but no one mentions it; everyone behaves as though it's normal, y' know inevitable that there's vandalism an' violence an' houses burnt out an' wrecked by the people they were built for. There's somethin' wrong. An' like the worst thing is that y' know the people who are supposed to like represent the people on our estate, y' know the *Daily Mirror* an' *The Sun*, an' ITV an' the Unions, what are they tellin' people to do? They just tell them to go out an' get more money, don't they? But they don't want more money; it's like me, isn't it? Y' know, buyin' new dresses all the time, isn't it? The Unions tell them to go out an' get more money an' ITV an' the papers tell them what to spend it on so the disease is always covered up.

Frank swivels round in his chair to face Rita

Frank *(after a pause)* Why didn't you take a course in politics?

Rita Politics? Go way, I hate politics. I'm just tellin' y' about round our way. I wanna be on this course findin' out. You know what I learn from you, about art an' literature, it feeds me, inside. I can get through the rest of the week if I know I've got comin' here to look forward to. Denny tried to stop me comin' tonight. He tried to get me to go out to the pub with him an' his mates. He hates me comin' here. It's like drug addicts, isn't it? They hate it when one of them tries to break away. It makes me stronger comin' here. That's what Denny's frightened of.

Frank "Only connect."

Rita Oh, not friggin' Forster again.

Frank "Only connect." You see what you've been doing?

Rita Just tellin' y' about home.

disease illness **inevitable** [ɪnˈevɪtəbl] certain to happen; unavoidable **wrecked** destroyed **Daily Mirror/The Sun** popular papers similar to "Bildzeitung" **unions** Trades Unions; *G.* Gewerkschaften **papers** newspapers **drug addict** [ˈædɪkt] *G.* Rauschgiftsüchtiger **to break away** (suddenly) to stop doing, thinking or believing s.th.

Frank Yes, and connecting, your dresses/ITV and the *Daily Mirror.* Addicts/you and your husband.

Frank Ogh!

Frank You see?

Rita An' – an' in that book – no-one does connect.

Frank Irony.

Rita Is that it? Is that all it means?

Frank Yes.

Rita Why didn't y' just tell me, right from the start?

Frank I could have told you; but you'll have a much better understanding of something if you discover it in your own terms.

Rita *(sincerely)* Aren't you clever?

Frank Brilliant. Now. *Peer Gynt.*

Rita All right, all right, hold on. *(She opens a couple of books and starts writing)*

Frank continues his marking and does not notice as Rita finishes writing. She picks up her chair, essay, pen and books, and moves across in front of his desk. She replaces the chair by the desk and stands watching him

Frank *(looking up)* What?

Rita I've done it.

Frank You've done it?

She hands him the essay

(Reading aloud) "In attempting to resolve the staging difficulties in a production of Ibsen's *Peer Gynt* I would present it on the radio because as Ibsen himself says, he wrote the play as a play for voices, never intending it to go on in a theatre. If they had the radio in his day that's where he would have done it."

He looks up as she beams him a satisfied smile

Black-out.

terms conditions **hold on** • wait a moment **to intend** to plan **to beam** to smile radiantly

Scene 5

As the Lights come up Frank is sitting in the swivel chair and Rita stands by the filing cabinet

Frank What's wrong? *(After a pause)* You know this is getting to be a bit wearisome. When you come to this room you'll do anything except start work immediately. Couldn't you just come in prepared to start work? Where's your essay?

Rita *(staring out of the window)* I haven't got it.

Frank You haven't done it?

Rita I said I haven't got it.

Frank You've lost it?

Rita It's burnt.

Frank Burnt?

Rita So are all the Chekhov books you lent me. Denny found out I was on the pill again; it was my fault, I left me prescription out. He burnt all me books.

Frank Oh Christ!

Rita I'm sorry. I'll buy y' some more.

Frank I wasn't referring to the books. Sod the books.

Rita Why can't he just let me get on with me learnin'? You'd think I was havin' a bloody affair the way he behaves.

Frank And aren't you?

Rita wanders DR. *She fiddles with the library steps, smoothing the top step*

Rita *(looking at him)* No. What time have I got for an affair? I'm busy enough findin' meself, let alone findin' someone else. I don't want anyone else. I've begun to find me – an' it's great y' know, it is Frank. It might sound selfish but all I want for the time bein' is what I'm findin' inside me. I certainly don't wanna be rushin' off with some feller, cos the first thing I'll have to do is forget about meself for the sake of him.

Frank Perhaps, perhaps your husband thinks you're having an affair with me.

wearisome *G.* ermüdend, lästig **Chekhov** Anton Pavlovich Chekhov (1860–1904), Russian dramatist and short-story writer **to leave s.th. out** to leave s.th. lying around **prescription** written order for medicine given to a patient by a doctor **sod the books ▲** damn the books; never mind the books **to get on with** to continue **to fiddle with** to play with nervously and aimlessly **to smooth** [smu:ð] to stroke with the hand **selfish** egoistic **for the time being** at the moment **feller •** fellow; man **for the sake of him** for his benefit; because of him

Rita Oh go way. You're me teacher. I've told him.

Frank You've told him about me? What?

Rita *(sitting down)* I've – tch – I've tried to explain to him how you give me room to breathe. Y' just, like feed me without expectin' anythin' in return.

Frank What did he say?

Rita He didn't. I was out for a while. When I come back he'd burnt me books an' papers, most of them. I said to him, y' soft get, even if I was havin' an affair there's no point burnin' me books. I'm not havin' it off with Anton Chekhov. He said, "I wouldn't put it past you to shack up with a foreigner".

Frank *(after a pause)* What are you going to do?

Rita I'll order some new copies for y' an' do the essay again.

Frank I mean about your husband.

Rita *(standing up)* I've told him, I said, "There's no point cryin' over spilt milk, most of the books are gone, but if you touch my *Peer Gynt* I'll kill y'."

Frank Tch. Be serious.

Rita I was!

Frank Do you love him?

Rita *(after a pause)* I see him lookin' at me sometimes, an' I know what he's thinkin', I do y' know, he's wonderin' where the girl he married has gone to. He even brings me presents sometimes, hopin' that the presents'll make her come back. But she can't, because she's gone, an' I've taken her place.

Frank Do you want to abandon this course?

Rita No. No!

Frank When art and literature begin to take the place of life itself, perhaps it's time to ...

Rita *(emphatically)* But it's not takin' the place of life, it's providin' me with life itself. He wants to take life away from me; he wants me to stop rockin' the coffin, that's all. Comin' here, doin' this, it's given me more life than I've had in years, an' he should be able

like • so to speak **come** • came **y' soft get** ▲ you stupid fool **there's no point (in)** there's no reason to **to have it off with s.o.** ▲ to have sex with s.o. **I would not put it past you** I would consider you capable of doing s.th. disreputable or unusual **to shack up with s.o.** ▲ to live together with s.o. (while unmarried) **to cry over spilt milk** to regret that s.th. which has happened cannot be changed **to abandon** to give up completely **emphatically** forcefully **to provide s.o. with s.th.** to give s.o. s.th. **to rock the coffin** • *usual form:* to rock the boat, *i.e.* to do s.th. that stops the smooth progress of an undertaking; *G.* eine Sache gefährden

to see that. Well, if he doesn't want me when I'm alive I'm certainly not just gonna lie down an' die for him. I told him I'd only have a baby when I had choice. But he doesn't understand. He thinks we've got choice because we can go into a pub that sells eight different kinds of lager. He thinks we've got choice already: choice between Everton an' Liverpool, choosin' which washin' powder, choosin' between one lousy school an' the next, between lousy jobs or the dole, choosin' between *Stork* an' butter.

Frank Yes. Well, perhaps your husband ...

Rita No. I don't wanna talk about him. *(She comes to the front of the desk)* Why was Chekhov a comic genius?

Frank Rita. Don't you think that for tonight we could give the class a miss?

Rita No. I wanna know. I've got to do this. He can burn me books an' me papers but if it's all in me head he can't touch it. It's like that with you, isn't it? You've got it all inside.

Frank Let's leave it for tonight. Let's go to the pub and drink pots of *Guinness* and talk.

Rita I've got to do this, Frank. I've got to. I want to talk about Chekhov.

Frank We really should talk about you and Denny, my dear.

Rita I don't want to.

Frank *(after a pause)* All right. Chekhov.

Rita goes to the U *end of the desk and stands between the chair and the desk*

"C" for Chekhov.

He gets up and moves towards the bookcase, taking Rita's chair with him. He stands on the chair and begins rummaging on the top shelf, dropping some of the books on the floor. Rita turns to sit down and notices her chair has gone. She sees Frank and watches him as he finds a bottle of whisky hidden behind some books. He gets down and takes the whisky to the small table

We'll talk about Chekhov and pretend this is the pub.

Rita Why d' y' keep it stashed behind there?

Everton, Liverpool Premier Division Liverpool football teams **lousy** • terrible **the dole** *colloquial term for:* the money given by the State to the unemployed **Stork** a brand name for margarine **to give s.th. a miss** not to take or do s.th.; to leave s.th. out **pots of** a lot of **I've got to** I must **to pretend** to make believe that s.th. is true **to stash** to hide

Frank *(pouring the drinks)* A little arrangement I have with my immediate employers. It's called discretion. They didn't tell me to stop drinking, they told me to stop displaying the signs.

Rita *(climbing on to the chair to replace the books)* Do you actually like drinking?

Frank Oh yes. I love it. Absolutely no guilt at all about it.

Rita Know when you were a poet, Frank, did y' drink then?

Frank Some. Not as much as now. *(He takes a drink)* You see, the great thing about the booze is that it makes one believe that under all the talk one is actually saying something.

Rita Why did you stop bein' a poet?

Frank *(wagging his finger at her)* That is a pub question.

Rita Well. I thought we were pretendin' this was the pub. *(She gets down from the chair)*

Frank In which we would discuss Chekhov.

Rita Well he's second on the bill. You're on first. Go on, why did y' stop?

Frank I didn't stop, so much as realize I never was. I'd simply got it wrong, Rita. *(After a pause)* Instead of creating poetry I spent – oh – years and years trying to create literature. You see?

Rita *(replacing her chair* U *of the desk)* Well I thought that's what poets did.

Frank What? *(He gives Rita her drink)*

Rita Y' know, make literature. *(She perches on the small table)*

Frank *(shaking his head)* Poets shouldn't believe in literature.

Rita *(puzzled)* I don't understand that.

Frank You will. You will.

Rita Sometimes I wonder if I'll ever understand any of it. It's like startin' all over again, y' know with a different language. Know I read that Chekhov play an' I thought it was dead sad, it was tragic; people committin' suicide an' that Constantin kid 's tryin' to produce his masterpiece an' they're all laughin' at him? It's tragic. Then I read the blurb on it an' everyone's goin' on about Chekhov bein' a comic genius.

Frank Well, it's not comedy like – erm – well it's not stand-up comedy. Have you ever seen Chekhov in the theatre?

arrangement agreement **immediate** direct **discretion** [dɪ'skreʃn] G. Umsicht **to display** to show openly **signs** *here:* evidence **guilt** the feeling that you have done wrong **bill** *here:* list of entertainers in a theatre programme **to realize** to understand **to perch** to sit on the edge **Constantin** character in *The Seagull,* play by Anton Chekhov (1896) **blurb** brief information **stand-up** (of a comedian) telling a series of jokes in front of an audience

Rita No. Does he go?

Frank Have you ever been to the theatre?

Rita No.

Frank You should go.

Rita *(standing up)* Hey! Why don't we go tonight?

Frank Me? Go to the theatre? God no, I hate the theatre.

Rita Why the hell are y' sendin' me?

Frank Because you want to know.

Rita *(packing her things into her bag)* Well, you come with me.

Frank And how would I explain that to Julia?

Rita Just tell her y' comin' to the theatre with me.

Frank "Julia, I shall not be in for dinner as I am going to the theatre with ravishing Rita."

Rita Oh sod off.

Frank I'm being quite serious.

Rita Would she really be jealous?

Frank If she knew I was at the theatre with an irresistible thing like you? Rita, it would be deaf and dumb breakfasts for a week.

Rita Why?

Frank Why not?

Rita I dunno – I just thought ...

Frank *(pouring himself another drink)* Rita, ludicrous as it may seem to you, even a woman who possesses an M.A. is not above common jealousy.

Rita Well, what's she got to be jealous of me for? I'm not gonna try an' rape y' in the middle of *The Seagull*.

Frank What an awful pity. You could have made theatre exciting for me again.

Rita Come on, Frank. Come with me. Y' never tell the truth you, do y'?

Frank What d' y' mean?

Rita Y' don't; y' like evade it with jokes an' that, don't y'? Come on, come to the theatre with me. We'll have a laugh ...

Frank Will we?

ravishing enchanting; delightful **jealous** *G.* eifersüchtig **irresistible** *G.* unwiderstehlich **I dunno** • I don't know **ludicrous** ridiculous, absurd **what's she got to be jealous of me for?** what reason has she to be jealous of me? **to rape** to force sexual intercourse on s.o. **what an awful pity** how very unfortunate **to evade** to find a way of not doing s.th.

Rita Yeh. C'mon we'll ring Julia. *(She goes to the telephone and picks up the receiver)*

Frank What!

Rita C'mon, what's your number?

Frank *(taking the receiver from her and replacing it)* We will not ring Julia. Anyway Julia's out tonight.

Rita So what will you do, spend the night in the pub?

Frank Yes.

Rita Come with me, Frank, y'll have a better time than y' will in the pub.

Frank Will I?

Rita Course y' will. *(She goes and gets both coats from the hook by the door, comes back and throws her coat over the back of the chair)*

Frank *(putting down his mug on the bookcase)* What is it you want to see?

Rita helps Frank into his coat

Rita *The Importance of Bein' Thingy* ...

Frank But *The Importance* isn't playing at the moment ...

Rita It is – I passed the church hall on the bus an' there was a poster ...

Frank breaks loose, turns to her and throws off his coat

Frank *(aghast)* An amateur production?

Rita What?

Frank Are you suggesting I miss a night at the pub to watch *The Importance* played by amateurs in a church hall?

Rita picks his coat up and puts it round his shoulders

Rita Yeh. It doesn't matter who's doin' it, does it? It's the same play, isn't it?

Frank Possibly, Rita ... *(He switches off the desk lamp)*

Rita *(putting on her coat and picking up her bag)* Well come on – hurry up – I'm dead excited. I've never seen a live play before.

Frank goes round switching off the electric fire and desk lamp and then picks up his briefcase

Frank And there's no guarantee you'll see a "live" play tonight.

Rita Why? Just cos they're amateurs? Y've gorra give them a chance. They have to learn somewhere. An' they might be good.

course • of course ***The Importance of Bein' Thingy*** *The Importance of Being Earnest* – well-known play by Oscar Wilde (1895). Thingy *cf. G.* "Dingsda" **aghast** [əˈgɑːst] amazed and terrified **gorra** • got to; must

Frank *(doubtfully)* Yes ...

Rita Oh y' an awful snob, aren't y'?

Frank *(smiling acknowledgement)* All right – come on.

They go towards the door

Rita Have you seen it before?

Frank Of course.

Rita Well, don't go tellin' me what happens will y'? Don't go spoilin' it for me.

Frank switches off the light switch. Black-out

Frank and Rita exit

Scene 6

The Lights come up

Frank enters carrying a briefcase and a pile of essays. He goes to the filing cabinet, takes his lecture notes from the briefcase and puts them in a drawer. He takes the sandwiches and apple from his briefcase and puts them on his desk and then goes to the window-desk and dumps the essays and briefcase. He switches on the radio and then sits in the swivel chair. He opens the packet of sandwiches, takes a bite and then picks up a book and starts reading

Rita bursts through the door out of breath

Frank What are you doing here? *(He looks at his watch)* It's Thursday, you ...

Rita *(moving over to the desk; quickly)* I know I shouldn't be here, it's me dinner hour, but listen, I've gorra tell someone, have y' got a few minutes, can y' spare ...?

Frank *(alarmed)* My God, what is it?

Rita I had to come an' tell y', Frank, last night, I went to the theatre! A proper one, a professional theatre.

Frank gets up and switches off the radio and then returns to the swivel chair

Frank *(sighing)* For God's sake, you had me worried, I thought it was something serious.

Rita No, listen, it was. I went out an' got me ticket, it was Shakespeare, I thought it was gonna be dead borin' ...

to spoil s.th. for s.o. to ruin s.o.'s pleasure in s.th. **lecture notes** *G.* Vorlesungsmanuskript **to spare (the time)** to find (the time) **to have s.o. worried** to make s.o. anxious

Frank Then why did you go in the first place?
Rita I wanted to find out. But listen, it wasn't borin', it was bleedin' great, honest, ogh, it done me in, it was fantastic. I'm gonna do an essay on it.
Frank *(smiling)* Come on, which one was it?
Rita moves URC
Rita "... Out, out, brief candle!
Life's but a walking shadow, a poor player
That struts and frets his hour upon the stage
And then is heard no more. It is a tale
Told by an idiot, full of sound and fury
Signifying nothing."
Frank *(deliberately)* Ah, *Romeo and Juliet.*
Rita *(moving towards Frank)* Tch. Frank! Be serious. I learnt that today from the book. *(She produces a copy of "Macbeth")* Look, I went out an' bought the book. Isn't it great? What I couldn't get over is how excitin' it was.
Frank puts his feet up on the desk
Wasn't his wife a cow, eh? An' that fantastic bit where he meets Macduff an' he thinks he's all invincible. I was on the edge of me seat at that bit. I wanted to shout out an' tell Macbeth, warn him.
Frank You didn't, did you?
Rita Nah. Y' can't do that in a theatre, can y'? It was dead good. It was like a thriller.
Frank Yes. You'll have to go and see more.
Rita I'm goin' to. *Macbeth*'s a tragedy, isn't it?
Frank nods
Right.
Rita smiles at Frank and he smiles back at her
Well I just – I just had to tell someone who'd understand.
Frank I'm honoured that you chose me.
Rita *(moving towards the door)* Well, I better get back. I've left a customer with a perm lotion. If I don't get a move on there'll be another tragedy.
Frank No. There won't be a tragedy.

to do s.o. in• *here:* to overwhelm s.o. **"Out, out, brief candle! ..."** famous quotation from the tragedy *Macbeth* (V. 5) by William Shakespeare **deliberately** slowly and carefully **bit** part **invincible** too strong to be defeated **I better (get back) •** I had better; I should (get back)

Rita There will, y' know. I know this woman; she's dead fussy. If her perm doesn't come out right there'll be blood an' guts everywhere.

Frank Which might be quite tragic –

He throws her the apple from his desk which she catches

– but it won't be a tragedy.

Rita What?

Frank Well – erm – look; the tragedy of the drama has nothing to do with the sort of tragic event you're talking about. Macbeth is flawed by his ambition – yes?

Rita *(going and sitting in the chair by the desk)* Yeh. Go on. *(She starts to eat the apple)*

Frank Erm – it's that flaw which forces him to take the inevitable steps towards his own doom. You see?

Rita offers him the can of soft drink. He takes it and looks at it

(Putting the can down on the desk) No thanks. Whereas, Rita, a woman's hair being reduced to an inch of stubble, or – or the sort of thing you read in the paper that's reported as being tragic, "Man Killed By Falling Tree", is not a tragedy.

Rita It is for the poor sod under the tree.

Frank Yes, it's tragic, absolutely tragic. But it's not a tragedy in the way that *Macbeth* is a tragedy. Tragedy in dramatic terms is inevitable, pre-ordained. Look, now, even without ever having heard the story of *Macbeth* you wanted to shout out, to warn him and prevent him going on, didn't you? But you wouldn't have been able to stop him would you?

Rita No.

Frank Why?

Rita They would have thrown me out the theatre.

Frank But what I mean is that your warning would have been ignored. He's warned in the play. But he can't go back. He still treads the path to doom. But the poor old fellow under the tree hasn't arrived there by following any inevitable steps has he?

Rita No.

Frank There's no particular flaw in his character that has dictated his end. If he'd been warned of the consequences of standing beneath

fussy (person) s.o. who attaches importance to unimportant details **to come out right** to be a success **guts** intestines; bowels; *G.* Eingeweide **blood and guts** • an unpleasant scene **to be flawed** to have an imperfection **inevitable** unavoidable **doom** ruin; death **pre-ordained** determined in advance **to tread** [tred] to walk on

that particular tree he wouldn't have done it, would he? Understand.

Rita So – so Macbeth brings it on himself?

Frank Yes. You see he goes blindly on and on and with every step he's spinning one more piece of thread which will eventually make up the network of his own tragedy. Do you see?

Rita I think so. I'm not used to thinkin' like this.

Frank It's quite easy, Rita.

Rita It is for you. I just thought it was a dead excitin' story. But the way you tell it you make me see all sorts of things in it. *(After a pause)* It's fun, tragedy, isn't it? *(She goes over to the window)* All them out there, they know all about that sort of thing don't they?

Frank Look, how about a proper lunch?

Rita Lunch? *(She leaps up, grabs the copy of "Macbeth", the can of drink and the apple and goes to the door)* Christ – me customer. She only wanted a demi-wave – she'll come out looking like a friggin' golliwog! *(She comes back to the table)* Ey' Frank, listen – I was thinkin' of goin' to the art gallery tomorrow. It's me half-day off. D' y' wonna come with me?

Frank *(smiling)* All right.

Rita goes to the door

(Looking at her) And – look, what are you doing on Saturday?

Rita I work.

Frank Well, when you finish work.

Rita Dunno.

Frank I want you to come over to the house.

Rita Why?

Frank Julia's organized a few people to come round for dinner.

Rita An' y' want me to come? Why?

Frank Why do you think?

Rita I dunno.

Frank Because you might enjoy it.

Rita Oh.

Frank Will you come?

Rita If y' want.

Frank What do you want?

Rita All right. I'll come.

to bring s.th. on to cause s.th. to happen **thread** *G.* Faden **network** complex system **them (students)** • those (students) **friggin'** ▲ *G. etwa:* verdammt **golliwog** ['gɒlɪwɒg] a black-faced doll with thick stiff hair

Frank Will you bring Denny?
Rita I don't know if he'll come.
Frank Well ask him.
Rita *(puzzled)* All right.
Frank What's wrong?
Rita What shall I wear?
Black-out
Rita goes out

Scene 7

The Lights come up on Frank who is sitting in the armchair listening to the radio
Rita enters, goes straight to the desk and slings her bag on the back of her chair
She sits in the chair and unpacks the note-pad and pencil-case from her bag. She opens the pad and takes out the pencil-sharpener and pencils and arranges them as before. Frank gets up, switches off the radio, goes to the swivel chair and sits

Frank Now I don't mind; two empty seats at the dinner table means more of the vino for me. But Julia – Julia is the stage-manager type. If we're having eight people to dinner she expects to see eight. She likes order – probably why she took me on – it gives her a lot of practice –
Rita starts sharpening her pencils
– and having to cope with six instead of eight was extremely hard on Julia. I'm not saying that I needed any sort of apology; you don't turn up that's up to you, but ...
Rita I did apologize.
Frank "Sorry couldn't come", scribbled on the back of your essay and thrust through the letter box? Rita, that's hardly an apology.
Rita What does the word "sorry" mean if it's not an apology? When I told Denny we were goin' to yours he went mad. We had a big fight about it.

to sling to throw carelessly **vino** wine **stage-manager** *here:* organizer **to take s.o. on** to accept s.o. (as an opponent) **to cope** to manage successfully **to be hard on s.o.** to ask too much of s.o.; to be unnecessarily severe **to turn up** • to arrive **that's up to you** that's your decision **to thrust** to push violently

Frank I'm sorry. I didn't realize. But look, couldn't you have explained? Couldn't you have said that was the reason?

Rita No. Cos that wasn't the reason. I told Denny if he wasn't gonna go I'd go on me own. An' I tried to. All day Saturday, all day in the shop I was thinkin' what to wear. I got back, an' I tried on five different dresses. They all looked bleedin' awful. An' all the time I'm trying to think of things I can say, what I can talk about. An' I can't remember anythin'. It's all jumbled up in me head. I can't remember if it's Wilde who's witty an' Shaw who was Shavian or who the hell wrote *Howards End.*

Frank Ogh God!

Rita Then I got the wrong bus to your house. It took me ages to find it. Then I walked up your drive, an' I saw y' all through the window, y' were sippin' drinks an' talkin' an' laughin'. An' I couldn't come in.

Frank Of course you could.

Rita I couldn't. I'd bought the wrong sort of wine. When I was in the off-licence I knew I was buyin' the wrong stuff. But I didn't know which was the right wine.

Frank Rita for Christ's sake; I wanted *you* to come along. You weren't expected to dress up or buy wine.

Rita *(holding all the pencils and pens in her hands and playing with them)* If you go out to dinner don't you dress up? Don't you take wine?

Frank Yes, but ...

Rita Well?

Frank Well what?

Rita Well you wouldn't take sweet sparkling wine, would y'?

Frank Does it matter what I do? It wouldn't have mattered if you'd walked in with a bottle of Spanish plonk.

Rita It was Spanish.

Frank Why couldn't you relax? *(He gets up and goes behind Rita's chair, then leans on the back of it)* It wasn't a fancy dress party. You could have come as yourself. Don't you realize how people would have seen you if you'd just – just breezed in? Mm? They would have seen someone who's funny, delightful, charming ...

to jumble up to mix up **Shaw** George Bernard Shaw (1856–1950), Irish dramatist and critic **Shavian** [ˈʃeivɪən] in the manner of Shaw; devotee of Shaw **ages** a very long time **drive** *G.* die Zufahrt **to sip** to drink very small quantities **off-licence** shop where alcohol is sold to be taken away **sparkling wine** *G.* Schaumwein **plonk** • cheap, poor quality wine **fancy dress** unusual costume **to breeze in** to enter unexpectedly in a happy way

Rita *(angrily)* But I don't wanna be charming and delightful: funny. What's funny? I don't wanna be funny. I wanna talk seriously with the rest of you, I don't wanna spend the night takin' the piss, comin' on with the funnies because that's the only way I can get into the conversation. I didn't want to come to your house just to play the court jester.

Frank You weren't being asked to play that role. I just – just wanted you to be yourself.

Rita But I don't want to be myself. Me? What's me? Some stupid woman who gives us all a laugh because she thinks she can learn, because she thinks that one day she'll be like the rest of them, talking seriously, confidently, with knowledge, livin' a civilized life. Well, she can't be like that really but bring her in because she's good for a laugh!

Frank If you believe that that's why you were invited, to be laughed at, then you can get out, now. *(He goes to his desk and grabs the pile of essays, taking them to the window desk. He stands with his back to Rita and starts pushing the essays into his briefcase)* You were invited because I wished to have your company and if you can't believe that then I suggest you stop visiting me and start visiting an analyst who can cope with paranoia.

Rita I'm all right with you, here in this room; but when I saw those people you were with I couldn't come in. I would have seized up. Because I'm a freak. I can't talk to the people I live with anymore. An' I can't talk to the likes of them on Saturday, or them out there, because I can't learn the language. I'm a half-caste. I went back to the pub where Denny was, an' me mother, an' our Sandra, an' her mates. I'd decided I wasn't comin' here again.

Frank turns to face her

I went into the pub an' they were singin', all of them singin' some song they'd learnt from the juke-box. An' I stood in that pub an' thought, just what the frig am I trying to do? Why don't I just pack it in an' stay with them, an' join in the singin'?

Frank And why don't you?

funnies • jokes **court jester** a man whose job used to be to amuse the king and his household; *G.* Hofnarr **to be good for a laugh** person or thing not taken seriously and laughed at **to get out** • to leave **to grab** to take roughly; to snatch **paranoia** [ˌpærəˈnɔɪə] mental disorder involving a feeling of persecution **freak** abnormal person **the likes of them** • people like them **half-caste** [kɑːst] *G.* Mischling; Halbblut **mates** • friends; *G.* Kumpel **juke-box** coin-operated record-player (usually in a public place) **what the frig?** ▲ what on earth? **to pack s.th. in** • to give s.th. up

Rita *(angrily)* You think I can, don't you? Just because you pass a pub doorway an' hear the singin' you think we're all O.K., that we're all survivin', with the spirit intact. Well I did join in with the singin', I didn't ask any questions, I just went along with it. But when I looked round me mother had stopped singin', an' she was cryin', but no-one could get it out of her why she was cryin'. Everyone just said she was pissed an' we should get her home. So we did, an' on the way I asked her why. I said, "Why are y' cryin', Mother?" She said, "Because – because we could sing better songs than those." Ten minutes later, Denny had her laughing and singing again, pretending she hadn't said it. But she had. And that's why I came back. And that's why I'm staying.

Black-out

Rita goes out

Scene 8

The Lights come up on Frank seated in the swivel chair at the desk reading Rita's "Macbeth" essay

Rita enters slowly, carrying a suitcase

Frank *(without looking up)* One second.

She puts down the suitcase RC *and wanders slowly* R *with her back to Frank*

(He closes the essay he has been reading, sighs and removes his glasses)

Your essay. *(He sees the suitcase)* What's that?

Rita It's me case.

Frank Where are you going?

Rita Me mother's.

Frank What's wrong? *(After a pause)* Rita!

Rita I got home from work, he'd packed me case. He said either I stop comin' here an' come off the pill or I could get out altogether.

Frank Tch.

Rita It was an ultimatum. I explained to him. I didn't get narked or anythin'. I just explained to him how I had to do this. He said it's warped me. He said I'd betrayed him. I suppose I have.

intact undamaged; complete **narked** • annoyed; angry **to warp** to distort **to betray** to be deceitful and disloyal

Frank Why have you?

Rita I have. I know he's right. But I couldn't betray meself. *(After a pause)* He says there's a time for education. An' it's not when y' twenty-six an' married.

Frank gets up and goes towards Rita who still faces away from him

Frank *(after a pause)* Where are you going to stay?

Rita I phoned me mother; she said I could go there for a week. Then I'll get a flat. *(She starts to cry)* I'm sorry, it's just ...

Frank takes hold of her and tries to guide her to the chair DR

Frank Look, come on, sit down.

Rita *(breaking away from him)* It's all right – I'll be O.K. Just give me a minute. *(She dries her eyes)* What was me *Macbeth* essay like?

Frank Oh sod *Macbeth*.

Rita Why?

Frank Rita!

Rita No, come on, come on, I want y' to tell me what y' thought about it.

Frank In the circumstances ...

Rita *(going and hanging her bag on the back of the swivel chair)* It doesn't matter, it doesn't; in the circumstances I need to go on, to talk about it an' do it. What was it like? I told y' it was no good. Is it really useless?

Frank sits in the chair DR

Frank *(sighing)* I – I really don't know what to say.

Rita Well try an' think of somethin'. Go on, I don't mind if y' tell me it was rubbish. I don't want pity, Frank. Was it rubbish?

Frank No, no. It's not rubbish. It's a totally honest, passionate account of your reaction to a play. It's an unashamedly emotional statement about a certain experience.

Rita Sentimental?

Frank No. It's too honest for that. It's almost – erm – moving. But in terms of what you're asking me to teach you of passing exams ... Oh, God, you see, I don't ...

Rita Say it, go on, say it!

Frank In those terms it's worthless. It shouldn't be, but it is; in its own terms it's – it's wonderful.

Oh sod Macbeth ▲ to hell with Macbeth **account** description **unashamedly** totally open and frank

Rita *(confronting him across the desk)* It's worthless! You said. An' if it's worthless you've got to tell me because I wanna write essays like those on there. *(She points to the essays on the desk)* I wanna know, an' pass exams like they do.

Frank But if you're going to write this sort of stuff you're going to have to change.

Rita All right. Tell me how to do it.

Frank *(getting up)* But I don't know if I want to tell you, Rita, I don't know that I want to teach you. *(He moves towards the desk)* What you already have is valuable.

Rita Valuable? What's valuable? The only thing I value is here, comin' here once a week.

Frank But, don't you see, if you're going to write this sort of thing – *(he indicates the pile of essays)* – to pass examinations, you're going to have to suppress, perhaps even abandon your uniqueness. I'm going to have to change you.

Rita But don't you realize, I want to change! Listen, is this your way of tellin' me that I can't do it? That I'm no good?

Frank It's not that at ...

Rita If that's what you're tryin' to tell me I'll go now ...

Frank turns away from her

Frank *(moving away from the desk)* No no no. Of course you're good enough.

Rita See I know it's difficult for y' with someone like me. But you've just gorra keep tellin' me an' then I'll start to take it in; y' see, with me you've got to be dead firm. You won't hurt me feelings y' know. If I do somethin' that's crap, I don't want pity, you just tell me, that's crap. *(She picks up the essay)* Here, it's crap. *(She rips it up)* Right. So we dump that in the bin, *(she does so)* an' we start again.

CURTAIN

to indicate to point to **to suppress** to try to put an end to **to abandon** to give up completely **uniqueness** *G.* Einzigartigkeit **to take s.th. in** • to understand **crap** ▲ rubbish **bin** container for rubbish; *here:* wastepaper basket

ACT II

SCENE 1

When the CURTAIN *rises Frank is sitting at his desk typing poetry. He pauses, stubs out a cigarette, takes a sip from the mug at his side, looks at his watch and then continues typing*

Rita bursts through the door. She is dressed in new, second-hand clothes

Rita Frank! *(She twirls on the spot to show off her new clothes)*

Frank *(smiling)* And what is this vision, returning from the city? *(He gets up and moves towards Rita)* Welcome back.

Rita Frank, it was fantastic.

She takes off her shawl and gives it to Frank who hangs it on the hook by the door. Rita goes to the desk

(Putting down her bag on the desk) Honest, it was – ogh!

to stub out a cigarette to extinguish a cigarette by pressing it against s.th. **to twirl** to turn round and round **shawl** a large piece of material worn about the shoulders

Frank What are you talking about, London or summer school?

Rita Both. A crowd of us stuck together all week. We had a great time: dead late every night, we stayed up talkin', we went all round London, got drunk, went to the theatres, bought all sorts of second-hand gear in the markets ... Ogh, it was ...

Frank So you won't have had time to do any actual work there?

Rita Work? We never stopped. Lashin' us with it they were; another essay, lash, do it again, lash.

Frank moves towards the desk

Another lecture, smack. It was dead good though. *(She goes and perches on the bookcase* UR*)*

Frank sits in the swivel chair, facing her

Y' know at first I was dead scared. I didn't know anyone. I was gonna come home. But the first afternoon I was standin' in this library, y' know lookin' at the books, pretendin' I was dead clever. Anyway, this tutor come up to me, he looked at the book in me hand an' he said, "Ah, are you fond of Ferlinghetti?" It was right on the tip of me tongue to say, "Only when it's served with Parmesan cheese", but, Frank, I didn't. I held it back an' I heard meself sayin', "Actually, I'm not too familiar with the American poets". Frank, you woulda been dead proud of me. He started talkin' to me about the American poets – we sat around for ages – an' he wasn't even one of my official tutors, y' know. We had to go to this big hall for a lecture, there must have been two thousand of us in there. After he'd finished his lecture this professor asked if anyone had a question, an', Frank, I stood up! *(She stands)* Honest to God, I stood up, an' everyone's lookin' at me. I don't know what possessed me, I was gonna sit down again, but two thousand people had seen me stand up, so I did it, I asked him the question.

There is a pause and Frank waits

Frank Well?

Rita Well what?

Frank What was the question?

summer school course of lectures, often at a university, during the summer vacation **to stick together** • to be/remain friends **gear** • clothes **to lash** • to beat; to whip **smack** *G.* klatsch! **scared** frightened **Ferlinghetti** Lawrence Ferlinghetti (born 1919), New York poet living in San Francisco – identified with the Beat Movement **honest to God** • honestly **what possessed me** what influenced me; what made me do it

Rita Oh, I dunno, I forget now, cos after that I was askin' questions all week, y' couldn't keep me down. I think that first question was about Chekhov; cos y' know I'm dead familiar with Chekhov now.

He smiles. Rita moves to the chair by the desk and sits. Frank swivels round to face her

Hey, what was France like? Go on, tell us all about it.

Frank There isn't a lot to tell.

Rita Ah go on, tell me about it; I've never been abroad. Tell me what it was like.

Frank Well – it was rather hot ... *(He offers her a "Gauloise")*

Rita No, ta, I've packed it in. Did y' drink?

Frank Ah – a little. *(He puts the cigarettes on the table)*

Rita Tch. Did y' write?

Frank A little.

Rita Will y' show it to me?

Frank Perhaps ... One day, perhaps.

Rita So y' wrote a bit an' y' drank a bit? Is that all?

Frank *(in a matter of fact tone)* Julia left me.

Rita What?

Frank Yes. But not because of the obvious, oh no – it had nothing whatsoever to do with the ratatouille. It was actually caused by something called *œufs en cocotte*.

Rita What?

Frank Eggs, my dear, eggs. Nature in her wisdom cursed me with a dislike for the egg be it cocotte, Florentine, Benedict or plain hardboiled. Julia insisted that nature was wrong. I defended nature and Julia left.

Rita Because of eggs?

Frank Well – let's say that it began with eggs. *(He packs away the typewriter)* Anyway, that's most of what happened in France. Anyway, the holiday's over, you're back, even Julia's back.

Rita Is she? Is it all right?

Frank *(putting the typewriter on the window desk and the sheets of poetry in the top left drawer)* Perfect. I get the feeling we shall stay together forever; or until she discovers *œufs à la crécy*.

to keep s.o. down • to stop s.o.; to control s.o.'s enthusiasm **Gauloise** a brand name for a French cigarette **matter of fact** non-emotional **wisdom** *G.* Weisheit **to curse** *here:* to punish **œufs en cocotte, Florentine, Benedict** eggs prepared and served in different ways, *e.g.* Eggs Benedict are poached eggs on a slice of tongue, served with sauce Mornay (cheese sauce)

Rita *Œufs à la crécy?* Does that mean eggs? Trish was goin' on about those; is that all it is, eggs?

Frank Trish?

Rita Trish, me flatmate, Trish. God is it that long since I've seen y', Frank? She moved into the flat with me just before I went to summer school.

Frank Ah. Is she a good flatmate?

Rita She's great. Y' know she's dead classy. Y' know like, she's got taste, y' know like you, Frank, she's just got it. Everything in the flat's dead unpretentious, just books an' plants everywhere. D' y' know somethin', Frank? I'm havin' the time of me life; I am y' know. I even feel – *(moving to the window)* – I feel young, you know like them down there.

Frank My dear, twenty-six is hardly old.

Rita I know that; but I mean, I feel young like them ... I can be young. *(She goes to her bag)* Oh listen – *(she puts the bag on the desk and rummages in it, producing a box)* – I bought y' a present back from London – it isn't much but I thought ...

She gives him a small box

Here.

Frank puts on his glasses, gets the scissors out of the pot on the desk, cuts the string and opens the box to reveal an expensive pen

Rita See what it says – it's engraved.

Frank *(reading)* "Must only be used for poetry. By strictest order – Rita" ... *(He looks up at her)*

Rita I thought it'd be like a gentle hint.

Frank Gentle?

Rita Every time y' try an' write a letter or a note with that pen, it won't work; you'll read that inscription an' it'll make you feel dead guilty – cos y' not writing poetry. *(She smiles at him)*

Frank *(getting up and pecking her on the cheek)* Thank you – Rita. *(He sits down again)*

Rita It's a pleasure. Come on. *(She claps her hands)* What are we doin' this term? Let's do a dead good poet. Come on, let's go an' have the tutorial down there.

Frank *(appalled)* Down where?

Trish short form of Patricia **flatmate** person who shares a flat **classy** • stylish; superior **unpretentious** modest; not trying to impress **hint** indirect suggestion **inscription** *G.* Inschrift **to peck** *here:* to kiss lightly and hurriedly **tutorial** period of group or individual instruction given by a university teacher

Rita *(getting her bag)* Down there – on the grass – come on.

Frank On the grass? Nobody sits out there at this time of year.

Rita They do – *(looking out of the window)* – there's some of them out there now.

Frank Well they'll have wet bums.

Rita What's a wet bum. You can sit on a bench. *(She tries to pull him to his feet)* Come on.

Frank *(remaining sitting)* Rita, I absolutely protest.

Rita Why?

Frank Like Dracula, I have an aversion to sunlight.

Rita Tch. *(She sighs)* All right. *(She goes to the window)* Let's open a window.

Frank If you must open a window then go on, open it. *(He swivels round to watch her)*

Rita *(struggling to open the window)* It won't bleedin' budge.

Frank I'm not surprised, my dear. It hasn't been opened for generations.

Rita *(abandoning it)* Tch. Y' need air in here, Frank. The room needs airing. *(She goes and opens the door)*

Frank This room does not need air, thank you very much.

Rita Course it does. A room is like a plant.

Frank A room is like a plant?

Rita Yeh, it needs air. *(She goes to her chair by the desk and sits)*

Frank And water, too, presumably? *(He gets up and closes the door)* If you're going to make an analogy why don't we take it the whole way? Let's get a watering-can and water the carpet; bring in two tons of soil and a bag of fertilizer. Maybe we could take cuttings and germinate other little rooms.

Rita Go way, you're mental you are.

Frank You said it, distinctly, you said, a room is like a plant.

Rita Well!

There is a pause

Frank Well what?

Rita Well any analogy will break down eventually.

bum • part of the body on which one sits **to struggle** to make a violent effort to do s.th. **to budge** • to move **to air** *G.* lüften **soil** earth **fertilizer** *G.* Düngemittel **cuttings** short pieces of a plant stem used for growing new plants **to germinate** to begin to grow **analogy** statement showing similarities between two different things with similar traits or properties

Frank Yes. And some will break down sooner than others. *(He smiles, goes to the bookcase* UL *and begins searching among the books)* Look, come on ... A great poet you wanted – well – we have one on the course ...

Rita sits on the desk watching Frank

I was going to introduce you to him earlier. *(As he rummages a book falls to one side revealing a bottle of whisky which has been hidden behind it)* Now – where is he ...?

Rita goes over and picks up the whisky bottle from the shelf

Rita Are you still on this stuff?

Frank Did I ever say I wasn't?

Rita *(putting the bottle down and moving away)* No. But ...

Frank But what?

Rita Why d' y' do it when y've got so much goin' for y', Frank?

Frank It is indeed because I have "so much goin' for me" that I do it. Life is such a rich and frantic whirl that I need the drink to help me step delicately through it.

Rita It'll kill y', Frank.

Frank Rita, I thought you weren't interested in reforming me.

Rita I'm not. It's just ...

Frank What?

Rita Just that I thought you'd started reforming yourself.

Frank Under your influence?

She shrugs

(He stops searching and turns to face her) Yes. But Rita – if I repent and reform, what do I do when your influence is no longer here? What do I do when, in appalling sobriety, I watch you walk away and disappear, my influence gone forever?

Rita Who says I'm gonna disappear?

Frank Oh you will, Rita. You've got to. *(He turns back to the shelves)*

Rita Why have I got to? This course could go on for years. An' when I've got through this one I might even get into the proper university here.

Frank And we'll all live happily ever after? Your going is as inevitable as – as ...

Rita *Macbeth*?

to search to look for or through **to have s.th. going for oneself •** to have many advantages **whirl** rapid succession of activities **to repent** [rɪ'pent] to wish one had not done s.th.; to be full of regret **sobriety** [sə'braɪətɪ] non-drunkenness; G. Nüchternheit

Frank *(smiling)* As tragedy, yes: but it will not be a tragedy, because I shall be glad to see you go.

Rita Tch. Thank you very much. *(After a pause)* Will y' really?

Frank Be glad to see you go? Well I certainly don't want to see you stay in a room like this for the rest of your life. Now. *(He continues searching for the book)*

Rita *(after a pause)* You can be a real misery sometimes, can't y'? I was dead happy a minute ago an' then you start an' make me feel like I'm having a bad night in a mortuary.

Frank finds the book he has been looking for and moves towards Rita with it

Frank Well here's something to cheer you up – here's our "dead good" poet – Blake.

Rita Blake? William Blake?

Frank The man himself. *You* will understand Blake; they over complicate him, Rita, but you will understand – you'll love the man.

Rita I know.

Frank What? *(He opens the book)* Look – look – read this ... *(He hands her the book and then goes and sits in the swivel chair)*

Rita looks at the poem on the page indicated and then looks at Frank

Rita *(reciting from memory)*

"O Rose, thou art sick!
The invisible worm
That flies in the night,
In the howling storm,
Has found out thy bed
Of crimson joy:
And his dark secret love
Does thy life destroy."

Frank You know it!

Rita *(laughing)* Yeh. *(She tosses the book on the desk and perches on the* UL *bookcase)* We did him at summer school.

Frank Blake at summer school? You weren't supposed to do Blake at summer school, were you?

misery • s.o. who is miserable/unhappy all the time **mortuary** ['mɔːtʃərɪ] place where dead bodies are kept before burial **to cheer s.o. up** to make s.o. happier **William Blake** English poet and mystic (1757–1827) **"O Rose ..."** poem by William Blake **to toss** to throw carelessly **to do s.o.** • to study an author, poet *etc.*

Rita Nah. We had this lecturer though, he was a real Blake freak. He was on about it every day. Everythin' he said, honest, everything was related to Blake – he couldn't get his dinner in the refectory without relating it to Blake – Blake and Chips. He was good though. On the last day we brought him a present, an' on it we put that poem, y' know, *The Sick Rose*. But we changed it about a bit; it was – erm –

"O Rose, thou aren't sick
Just mangled and dead
Since the rotten gardener
Pruned off thy head."

We thought he might be narked but he wasn't, he loved it. He said – what was it ...? He said, "Parody is merely a compliment masquerading as humour".

freak • odd or unusual person; *here:* fanatic **to be related to** to be connected with **refectory** college dining room **"O Rose ..."** parody of Blake's poem *G.* "Ach Rose, du krankst ja nicht! Bist tot und welk in deinem Topf, Weil der Gärtner, der blöde Tropf, Dir abgeschnitten hat den Kopf." **to masquerade as** [ˌmɑːskəˈreɪd] to pretend to be

Frank *(getting up und replacing the book on the shelf)* So ... you've already done Blake? You covered all the *Songs of Innocence and Experience*?

Rita Of course; you don't do Blake without doing innocence and experience, do y'?

Frank No. Of course. *(He goes and sits in the swivel chair)*

Black-out

Rita picks up her bag and shawl and exits

Scene 2

The Lights come up on Frank who is sitting at his desk marking an essay. Occasionally he makes a tutting sound and scribbles something. There is a knock at the door

Frank Come in.

Rita enters, closes the door, goes to the desk and dumps her bag on it. She takes her chair and places it next to Frank and sits down

Rita *(talking in a peculiar voice)* Hello, Frank.

Frank *(without looking up)* Hello. Rita, you're late.

Rita I know, Frank. I'm terribly sorry. It was unavoidable.

Frank *(looking up)* Was it really? What's wrong with your voice?

Rita Nothing is wrong with it, Frank. I have merely decided to talk properly. As Trish says there is not a lot of point in discussing beautiful literature in an ugly voice.

Frank You haven't got an ugly voice; at least you *didn't* have. Talk properly.

Rita I am talking properly. I have to practise constantly, in everyday situations.

Frank You mean you're going to talk like that for the rest of this tutorial?

Rita Trish says that no matter how difficult I may find it I must persevere.

Frank Well will you kindly tell Trish that I am not giving a tutorial

to cover to study all aspects of *Songs of Innocence and Experience* two series of poems by William Blake, the first expressing the all pervading presence of divine love, the second showing the power of evil **a tutting sound** a noise of disapproval **to scribble** to write quickly and carelessly **not a lot of point** • not much value **ugly** unpleasant **to persevere** [ˌpɜːsɪˈvɪə] to continue to try to be successful in s.th. which you find difficult

to a Dalek?

Rita I am not a Dalek.

Frank *(appealingly)* Rita, stop it!

Rita But Frank, I have to persevere in order that I shall.

Frank Rita! Just be yourself.

Rita *(reverting to her normal voice)* I am being myself. *(She gets up and moves the chair back to its usual place)*

Frank What's that?

Rita What?

Frank On your back.

Rita *(reaching up)* Oh – it's grass.

Frank Grass?

Rita Yeh, I got here early today. I started talking to some students down on the lawn. *(She sits in her usual chair)*

Frank You were talking to students – down there?

Rita *(laughing)* Don't sound so surprised. I can talk now y' know, Frank.

Frank I'm not surprised. Well! You used to be quite wary of them didn't you?

Rita God knows why. For students they don't half come out with some rubbish y' know.

Frank You're telling me?

Rita I only got talking to them in the first place because as I was walking past I heard one of them sayin' as a novel he preferred *Lady Chatterley* to *Sons and Lovers.* I thought, I can keep walkin' and ignore it, or I can put him straight. So I put him straight. I walked over an' said, "Excuse me but I couldn't help overhearin' the rubbish you were spoutin' about Lawrence". Shoulda seen the faces on them, Frank. I said tryin' to compare *Chatterley* with *Sons and Lovers* is like tryin' to compare sparkling wine with champagne. The next thing is there's this heated discussion, with me right in the middle of it.

Daleks robots in a cult TV science fiction series with distinctive metallic electronic voices **to revert to** to return (to a former condition) **to be wary of** to be cautious of; to be afraid of **to come out with** • to say s.th. without really thinking about the meaning **They don't half come out with some rubbish** • They really do say some stupid things **in the first place** at all *Lady Chatterley Lady Chatterley's Lover* – a novel by D.H. Lawrence (1928). This novel caused a scandal when first published **to put s.o. straight** • to explain to s.o. why his/her ideas are wrong **to overhear** to hear s.th. without meaning to listen **to spout** • [spaʊt] to speak at great length on a subject (without much content) **heated discussion** discussion in which people get very excited, even angry

Frank I thought you said the student claimed to "prefer" *Chatterley*, as a novel.

Rita He did.

Frank So he wasn't actually suggesting that it was superior.

Rita Not at first – but then he did. He walked right into it ...

Frank And so you finished him off, did you, Rita?

Rita Frank, he was askin' for it. He was an idiot. His argument just crumbled. It wasn't just me – everyone else agreed with me.

Frank returns to reading the essay

There was this really mad one with them; I've only been talkin' to them for five minutes and he's inviting me to go abroad with them all. They're all goin' to the South of France in the Christmas holidays, slummin' it.

Frank You can't go.

Rita What?

Frank You can't go – you've got your exams.

Rita My exams are before Christmas.

Frank Well – you've got your results to wait for ...

Rita Tch. I couldn't go anyway.

Frank Why? *(He looks at her)*

Rita It's all right for them. They *can* just jump into a bleedin' van an' go away. But I can't.

He returns to the essay

Tiger they call him, he's the mad one. His real name's Tyson but they call him Tiger.

Frank *(looking up)* Is there any point me going on with this? *(He points to the essay)*

Rita What?

Frank Is there much point in working towards an examination if you're going to fall in love and set off for the South of ...

Rita *(shocked)* What! Fall in love? With who? My God, Frank, I've just been talkin' to some students. I've heard of match-making but this is ridiculous.

Frank All right, but please stop burbling on about Mr Tyson.

Rita I haven't been burbling on.

He returns to the essay

to finish s.o. off • to defeat s.o. **to ask for it** • to lay oneself open to criticism **to crumble** to break into little pieces **to slum it** • to live intentionally below one's own standard of living **van** vehicle used for carrying and delivering goods **match-making** speculating on marriage partners for other people **to burble on** • to talk non-stop nonsense

What's it like?

Frank Oh – it – erm – wouldn't look out of place with these. *(He places it on top of a pile of other essays on his desk)*

Rita Honest?

Frank Dead honest.

Black-out

Frank exits

Scene 3

The Lights come up on Rita who is sitting in the armchair by the window, reading a heavy tome. There is the sound of muffled oaths from behind the door

Frank enters carrying his briefcase. He is very drunk

Frank Sod them – no, fuck them! Fuck them, eh, Rita? *(He goes to the desk)*

Rita Who?

Frank You'd tell them wouldn't you? You'd tell them where to get off. *(He gets a bottle of whisky from his briefcase)*

Rita Tell who, Frank?

Frank Yes – students – students reported me! *(He goes to the bookcase* UR *and puts the whisky on the shelf)* Me! Complained – you know something? They complained and it was the best lecture I've ever given.

Rita Were you pissed?

Frank Pissed? I was glorious! Fell off the rostrum twice. *(He comes round to the front of his desk)*

Rita Will they sack you?

Frank *(lying flat on the floor)* The sack? God no; that would involve making a decision. Pissed is all right. To get the sack it'd have to be rape on a grand scale; and not just the students either.

Rita gets up and moves across to look at him

to look out of place to be unsuitable, inappropriate **tome** a large or thick book **muffled** half-articulated **oaths** swear-words **to tell s.o. where to get off** ▲ *G.* jemandem die Meinung sagen **rostrum** [ˈrɒstrəm] platform for a public speaker **to sack s.o.** to dismiss s.o. from a job **to involve** *here:* to make necessary **grand scale** *here:* extremely frequently

That would only amount to a slight misdemeanour. For dismissal it'd have to be nothing less than buggering the bursar ... They suggested a sabbatical for a year – or ten ... Europe – or America ... I suggested that Australia might be more apt – the allusion was lost on them ...

Rita Tch. Frank, you're mad.

Frank Completely off my cake. I know.

Rita Even if y' don't think about yourself, what about the students?

Frank *What* about the students?

Rita Well it's hardly fair on them if their lecturer's so pissed that he's falling off the rostrum. *(She goes to her chair by the desk and replaces the book in her bag)*

Frank I might have fallen off, my dear, but I went down talking – and came up talking – never missed a syllable – what have they got to complain about?

Rita Maybe they did it for your own good.

Frank Or maybe they did it because they're a crowd of mealy-mouthed pricks who wouldn't know a poet if you beat them about the head with one. *(He half-sits up)* "Assonance" – I said to them – "Assonance means getting the rhyme wrong ..." *(He collapses back on to the floor again)* They looked at me as though I'd desecrated Wordsworth's tomb.

Rita Look, Frank, we'll talk about the Blake essay next week, eh?

Frank Where are you going? We've got a tutorial. *(He gets up and staggers towards her)*

Rita Frank, you're not in any fit state for a tutorial. I'll leave it with y' an' we can talk about it next week, eh?

Frank No – no – you must stay – erm ... Watch this – sober? *(He takes a huge breath and pulls himself together)* Sober! Come on ...

He takes hold of Rita and pushes her round the desk and sits her in the swivel chair

You can't go. I want to talk to you about this. *(He gets her essay and shows it to her)* Rita, what's this?

to amount to to add up to; to mean **slight** not serious **misdemeanour** ['mɪsdɪ'mi:nə] offence; breaking of the rules **to bugger** ▲ to commit sodomy; *G.* Analverkehr betreiben **bursar** ['bɜ:sə] treasurer of a college **sabbatical** [sə'bætɪkl] a year given to university teachers to enable them to undertake special studies **Australia** Britain used to send convicts into exile in Australia **apt** appropriate; suitable **off one's cake** mad; crazy **to do s.th. for s.o.'s own good** *G.* jemanden vor sich selbst schützen **mealy-mouthed** not wishing to speak plainly; insincere **prick** ▲ idiot **to desecrate** ['desɪkreɪt] to do profane things in a holy place; *G.* entweihen **Wordsworth** William Wordsworth, a famous English Romantic poet (1770–1850) **fit** suitable **state** condition **sober** ['səʊbə] not drunk

Rita Is there something wrong with it?

Frank It's just, look, this passage about *The Blossom* you seem to assume that the poem is about sexuality.

Rita It is!

Frank Is it?

Rita Well it's certainly a like richer poem, isn't it? If it's interpreted in that way.

Frank Richer? Why richer? We discussed it. The poem is a simple, uncomplicated piece about blossom, as if seen from a child's point of view.

Rita *(shrugging)* In one sense. But it's like, like the poem about the rose, isn't it? It becomes a more rewarding poem when you see that it works on a number of levels.

Frank Rita, *The Blossom* is a simple uncomplicated ...

Rita Yeh, that's what you say, Frank; but Trish and me and some others were talkin' the other night, about Blake, an' what came out of our discussion was that apart from the simple surface value of Blake's poetry there's always a like erm – erm –

Frank Well? Go on ...

Rita *(managing to)* – a like vein. Of concealed meaning. I mean if that poem's only about the blossom then it's not much of a poem is it?

Frank So? You think it gains from being interpreted in this way?

Rita *(slightly defiantly)* Is me essay wrong then, Frank?

Frank It's not – not wrong. But I don't like it.

Rita You're being subjective.

Frank *(half laughing)* Yes – yes I suppose I am. *(He goes slowly to the chair* UC *of the desk and sits down heavily)*

Rita If it was in an exam what sort of mark would it get?

Frank A good one.

Rita Well what the hell are you sayin' then?

Frank *(shrugging)* What I'm saying is that it's up to the minute, quite acceptable, trendy stuff about Blake; but there's nothing of you in there.

Rita Or maybe Frank, y' mean there's nothing of your views in there.

Frank *(after a pause)* Maybe that is what I mean?

rewarding satisfying **to work** *here:* can be interpreted **to come out** to emerge; to appear **vein** a coloured line in some sorts of stone *e.g.* marble; G. Ader, Maser **concealed** hidden **not much of a** not a very good **to gain** to improve **trendy** fashionable

Rita But when I first came to you, Frank, you didn't give me any views. You let me find my own.

Frank *(gently)* And your views I still value. But, Rita, these aren't your views.

Rita But you told me not to have a view. You told me to be objective, to consult recognized authorities. Well that's what I've done; I've talked to other people, read other books an' after consultin' a wide variety of opinion I came up with those conclusions.

He looks at her

Frank *(after a pause)* Yes. All right.

Rita *(rattled)* Look, Frank, I don't have to go along one hundred per cent with your views on Blake y' know. I can have a mind of my own can't I?

Frank I sincerely hope so, my dear.

Rita And what's that supposed to mean?

Frank It means – it means be careful.

Rita jumps up and moves in towards Frank

Rita *(angrily)* What d' y' mean be careful? I can look after myself. Just cos I'm learnin', just cos I can do it now an' read what I wanna read an' understand without havin' to come runnin' to you every five minutes y' start tellin' me to be careful. *(She paces about)*

Frank Because – because *I* care for you – I want you to care for yourself.

Rita Tch. *(She goes right up to Frank. After a pause)* I – I care for you, Frank ... But you've got to – to leave me alone a bit. I'm not an idiot now, Frank – I don't need you to hold me hand as much ... I can – I can do things on me own more now ... And I am careful. I know what I'm doin'. Just don't – don't keep treatin' me as though I'm the same as when I first walked in here. I understand now, Frank; I know the difference between – between – Somerset Maugham an' Harold Robbins. An' you're still treating me as though I'm hung up on *Rubyfruit Jungle. (She goes to the swivel chair and sits)* Just ... You understand, don't you Frank?

Frank Entirely, my dear.

Rita I'm sorry.

Frank Not at all. *(After a pause)* I got around to reading it you know, *Rubyfruit Jungle.* It's excellent.

to value to have a high opinion of **to come up with •** to find; to reach **to be hung up on •** to be emotionally disturbed by; to have a complex about **entirely** absolutely

Rita *(laughing)* Oh go way, Frank. Of its type it's quite interesting. But it's hardly excellence.

Black-out

Rita exits

Scene 4

The Lights come up on Frank sitting in the swivel chair

Rita enters and goes to the desk

Rita Frank ...

He looks at his watch

I know I'm late ... I'm sorry.

He gets up and moves away

Am I too late? We were talkin'. I didn't notice the time.

Frank Talking?

Rita Yeh. If it'll go in my favour we were talking about Shakespeare.

Frank Yes ... I'm sure you were.

Rita Am I too late then? All right. I'll be on time next week. I promise.

Frank Rita. Don't go.

Rita No – honestly, Frank – I know I've wasted your time. I'll see y' next week, eh?

Frank Rita! Sit down!

Rita goes to her usual chair and sits

(Going to the side of her) When you were so late I phoned the shop.

Rita Which shop?

Frank The hairdresser's shop. Where you work. Or, I should say, worked.

Rita I haven't worked there for a long time. I work in a bistro now.

Frank You didn't tell me.

Rita Didn't I? I thought I did. I was telling someone.

Frank It wasn't me.

Rita Oh. Sorry. *(After a pause)* What's wrong?

Frank *(after a pause)* It struck me that there was a time when you told me everything.

Rita I thought I had told you.

to go in s.o.'s favour to be to s.o.'s advantage **it struck me** the idea suddenly came to me

Frank No. Like a drink?

Rita Who cares if I've left hairdressin' to work in a bistro?

Frank I care. *(He goes* UR *to the bookshelves and takes a bottle from an eye-level shelf)* You don't want a drink? Mind if I do?

Rita But why do you care about details like that? It's just boring, insignificant detail.

Frank *(getting a mug from the small table)* Oh. Is it?

Rita That's why I couldn't stand being in a hairdresser's any longer; boring irrelevant detail all the time, on and on ... Well I'm sorry but I've had enough of that. I don't wanna talk about irrelevant rubbish anymore.

Frank And what do you talk about in your bistro? Cheers.

Rita Everything.

Frank Everything?

Rita Yeh.

Frank Ah.

Rita We talk about what's important, Frank, and we leave out the boring details for those who want them.

Frank Is Mr Tyson one of your customers?

Rita A lot of students come in; he's one of them. You're not gonna give me another warning are y', Frank?

Frank Would it do any good?

Rita Look, for your information I do find Tiger fascinatin', like I find a lot of the people I mix with fascinating; they're young, and they're passionate about things that matter. They're not trapped – they're too young for that. And I like to be with them.

Frank *(moving* DR *of the desk and keeping his back to her)* Perhaps – perhaps you don't want to waste your time coming here anymore?

Rita Don't be stupid. I'm sorry I was late. *(After a pause she gets up)* Look, Frank, I've got to go. I'm meeting Trish at seven. We're going to see a production of *The Seagull.*

Frank Yes. *(He turns to face her)* Well. When Chekhov calls ...

Rita Tch.

Frank You can hardly bear to spend a moment here can you?

Rita *(moving towards him a little)* That isn't true. It's just that I've got to go to the theatre.

to care to be interested **to mind** to object **to stand s.th.** to continue to accept; to endure **to mix with** to be in the company of **to be trapped** to be caught and unable to escape

Frank And last week you didn't turn up at all. Just a phone call to say you had to cancel.

Rita It's just that – that there's so many things happening now. It's harder.

Frank As I said, Rita, if you want to stop com –

Rita *(going right up to him)* For God's sake, I don't want to stop coming here. I've got to come here. What about my exam?

Frank Oh I wouldn't worry about that. You'd sail through it anyway. You really don't have to put in the odd appearance out of sentimentality; *(he moves round to the other side of the desk)* I'd rather you spared me that.

Frank goes to drink

Rita If you could stop pouring that junk down your throat in the hope that it'll make you feel like a poet you might be able to talk about things that matter instead of where I do or don't work; an' then it might be worth comin' here.

Frank Are you capable of recognizing what does or does not matter, Rita?

Rita I understand literary criticism, Frank. When I come here that's what we're supposed to be dealing with.

Frank You want literary criticism? *(He looks at her for a moment and then goes to the top drawer of his desk and takes out two slim volumes and some typewritten sheets of poetry and hands them to her)* I want an essay on that lot by next week.

Rita What is it?

Frank No sentimentality, no subjectivity. Just pure criticism. A critical assessment of a lesser known English poet. Me.

Black-out

Rita exits

to cancel to say that s.th. already arranged cannot take place **to sail through s.th.** to experience no difficulties **odd** *here:* occasional **to spare s.o. s.th.** not force s.o. to experience s.th. unpleasant; G. jmdm. etwas ersparen **junk** useless thing(s) **to be worth** to be of some value **slim** thin

Scene 5

The Lights come up on Frank sitting in a chair by the window-desk with a mug in his hand and a bottle of whisky on the desk in front of him listening to the radio. There is a knock at the door

Frank Come in.

Rita enters and goes to the swivel chair behind Frank's desk

(Getting up and switching off the radio) What the – what the hell are you doing here? I'm not seeing you till next week.

Rita Are you sober? Are you? nüchtern? → sober

Frank If you mean am I still this side of reasonable comprehension, then yes.

Rita *(going and standing next to him)* Because I want you to hear this when you're sober. *(She produces his poems)* These are brilliant. Frank, you've got to start writing again. *(She goes to the swivel chair and sits)* This is brilliant. They're witty. They're profound. Full of style.

Frank *(going to the small table and putting down his mug)* Ah ... tell me again, and again ...

Rita They are, Frank. It isn't only me who thinks so. Me an' Trish sat up last night and read them. She agrees with me. Why did you stop writing? Why did you stop when you can produce work like this? We stayed up most of the night, just talking about it. At first we just saw it as contemporary poetry in its own right, you know, as somethin' particular to this century but look, Frank, what makes it more – more ... What did Trish say –? More resonant than – purely contemporary poetry is that you can see in it a direct line through to nineteenth-century traditions of – of like wit an' classical allusion.

Frank *(going to the chair* U *of the desk and standing by the side of it)* Er – that's erm – that's marvellous, Rita. How fortunate I didn't let you see it earlier. Just think if I'd let you see it when you first came her.

Rita I know ... I wouldn't have understood it, Frank.

Frank You would have thrown it across the room and dismissed it as a heap of shit, wouldn't you?

witty clever and amusing **profound** with deep understanding or meaning **contemporary** of the present time

Rita *(laughing)* I know ... But I couldn't have understood it then, **Frank**, because I wouldn't have been able to recognize and understand the allusions.

Frank Oh I've done a fine job on you, haven't I.

Rita It's true, Frank. I can see now.

Frank You know, Rita, I think – I think that like you I shall change my name; from now on I shall insist upon being known as Mary, Mary Shelley – do you understand that allusion, Rita?

Rita What?

Frank She wrote a little Gothic number called *Frankenstein*.

Rita So?

Frank This – *(picking up his poetry and moving round to Rita)* – this clever, pyrotechnical pile of self-conscious allusion is worthless, talentless shit and could be recognized as such by anyone with a shred of common sense. It's the sort of thing that gives publishing a bad name. Wit? You'll find more wit in the telephone book, and, probably, more insight. Its one advantage over the telephone directory is that it's easier to rip. *(He rips the poems up and throws the pieces on to the desk)* It is pretentious, characterless and without style.

Rita It's not.

Frank Oh, I don't expect you to believe me, Rita; you recognize the hallmark of literature now, don't you? *(In a final gesture he throws a handful of the ripped pieces into the air and then goes to the chair* DR *and sits)* Why don't you just go away? I don't think I can bear it any longer.

Rita Can't bear what, Frank?

Frank You, my dear – you ...

Rita I'll tell you what you can't bear, Mr Self-Pitying Piss Artist; what you can't bear is that I am educated now. What's up, Frank, don't y' like me now that the little girl's grown up, now that y' can no longer bounce me on daddy's knee an' watch me stare back in wide-eyed wonder at everything he has to say? I'm educated, I've got what you have an' y' don't like it because you'd rather see me as the peasant I once was; you're like the rest of them – you

pyrotechnical [paɪrəˈteknɪkl] brilliant; *G.* feuerwerkartig **shred** a very little amount **to rip** to tear up **pretentious** claiming great worth without justification **hallmark** mark used by makers of gold and silver as a guarantee of quality **to bear s.th.** to tolerate s.th. **to bounce** to spring up and down, to cause to do this **peasant** • [ˈpeznt] *here:* ignorant person

like to keep your natives thick, because that way they still look charming and delightful. I don't need you. *(She gets up and picking up her bag moves away from the desk in the direction of the door)* I've got a room full of books. I know what clothes to wear, what wine to buy, what plays to see, what papers and books to read. I can do without you.

Frank Is that all you wanted. Have you come all this way for so very, very little?

Rita Oh it's little to you, isn't it? It's little to you who squanders every opportunity and mocks and takes it for granted.

Frank Found a culture have you, Rita? Found a better song to sing have you? No – you've found a different song, that's all – and on your lips it's shrill and hollow and tuneless. Oh, Rita, Rita ...

Rita Rita? *(She laughs)* Rita? Nobody calls me Rita but you. I dropped that pretentious crap as soon as I saw it for what it was. You stupid ... Nobody calls me Rita.

Frank What is it now then? Virginia?

Rita exits

Or Charlotte? Or Jane? Or Emily?

Black-out

Scene 6

The Lights come up on Frank talking into the telephone. He is leaning against the bookshelf

Frank Yes ... I think she works there ... Rita White ... No, no. Sorry. ... erm. What is it? ... Susan White? No? ... Thank you ... Thanks. ...

The Lights fade to Black-out to denote the passing of some time and then come up on Frank sitting at his desk with his back to the audience. He is drunk and talking on the telephone

Yes. ... Erm. ... Trish is it? ... Erm, yes I'm a friend of Rita's. ... Rita. ... I'm sorry Susan ... yes ... could you just say that – erm –

natives *here:* derogatory, allusion to primitive peoples with no western-style education **to squander** to waste **to take s.th. for granted** not appreciate s.th. when one has got it **shrill** sharp; highpitched **hollow** empty **Virginia, Charlotte, Jane, Emily** Virginia Woolf (1882–1941), Charlotte Brontë (1816–1855), Emily Brontë (1818–1848), Jane Austen (1775–1817) – four well-known English writers **to denote** to indicate

I've ... it's – erm – Frank here ... her tutor. ... Yes ... well could you tell her that I have – erm – I've entered her for her examination. ... Yes you see she doesn't know the details ... time and where the exam is being held. ... Could you tell her to call in? ... Please. ... Yes. ... Thank you.

The Lights fade to Black-out

Scene 7

The Lights come up

Rita enters and shuts the door. She is wrapped in a large winter coat. She lights a cigarette and moves across to the filing cabinet and places a Christmas card with the others already there. She throws the envelope in the waste-bin and opens the door revealing Frank with a couple of tea-chests either side of him. He is taken aback at seeing her and then he gathers himself and, picking up one of the chests, enters the room. Rita goes out to the corridor and brings in the other chest. Frank gets the chair from the U end of his desk and places it by the UL *bookcase. He stands on it and begins taking down the books from the shelves and putting them into the chests. Rita watches him but he continues as if she is not there*

Rita Merry Christmas, Frank. Have they sacked y'?

Frank Not quite.

Rita Well, why y' – packing your books away?

Frank Australia. *(After a pause)* Some weeks ago – made rather a night of it.

Rita Did y' bugger the bursar?

Frank Metaphorically. And as it was metaphorical the sentence was reduced from the sack to two years in Australia. Hardly a reduction in sentence really – but ...

Rita What did Julia say?

Frank *Bon voyage.*

Rita She's not goin' with y'?

Frank shakes his head. Rita begins helping him take down the books from the shelves and putting them in the chests

What y' gonna do?

chest large wooden box **to be taken aback** to be surprised, startled, shocked **to gather oneself** to compose oneself **sentence** punishment (given by a judge)

Frank What do you think I'll do? Aussie? It's a paradise for the likes of me.

Rita Tch. Come on, Frank ...

Frank It is. Didn't you know the Australians named their favourite drink after a literary figure? Forster's Lager they call it. Of course they get the spelling wrong – rather like you once did!

Rita Be serious.

Frank For God's sake, why did you come back here?

Rita I came to tell you you're a good teacher. *(After a pause)* Thanks for enterin' me for the exam.

Frank That's all right. I know how much it had come to mean to you.

Rita perches on the small table while Frank continues to take books from the upper shelves

Rita You didn't want me to take it, did y'? Eh? You woulda loved it if I'd written, "Frank knows all the answers", across me paper, wouldn't y'? I nearly did an' all. When the invigilator said, "Begin", I turned over me paper with the rest of them, and while they were all scribbling away against the clock, I just sat there, lookin' at the first question. Y' know what it was, Frank? "Suggest ways in which one might cope with some of the staging difficulties in a production of *Peer Gynt.*"

Frank gets down, sits on the chair and continues to pack the books

Frank Well, you should have had no trouble with that.

Rita I did though. I just sat lookin' at the paper an' thinkin' about what you'd said. I tried to ignore it, to pretend that you were wrong. You think you gave me nothing; did nothing for me. You think I just ended up with a load of quotes an' empty phrases; an' I did. But that wasn't your doin'. I was so hungry. I wanted it all so much that I didn't want it to be questioned. I told y' I was stupid. It's like Trish, y' know me flatmate, I thought she was so cool an' together – I came home the other night an' she'd tried to top herself. Magic, isn't it? She spends half her life eatin' wholefoods an' health foods to make her live longer, an' the other half tryin' to kill herself. *(After a pause)* I sat lookin' at the question, an' thinkin' about it all. Then I picked up me pen an' started.

Aussie • ['ɔzɪ] *slang word for:* Australian **the likes of** • people like **an' all** • as well; too **invigilator** [ɪn'vɪdʒɪleɪtə] person who organizes an examination in the examination room **cool an' together** • sophisticated and in control **to top o.s.** ▲ to commit suicide **wholefoods** biologically natural food products

Frank And you wrote, "Do it on the radio"?

Rita I could have done. An' you'd have been proud of me if I'd done that an' rushed back to tell you – wouldn't y'? But I chose not to. I had a choice. I did the exam.

Frank I know. A good pass as well.

Rita Yeh. An' it might be worthless in the end. But I had a choice. I chose, me. Because of what you'd given me I had a choice. I wanted to come back an' tell y' that. That y' a good teacher.

Frank *(stopping working and looking at her)* You know – erm – I hear very good things about Australia. Things are just beginning there. The thing is, why don't you – come as well? It'd be good for us to leave a place that's just finishing for one that's just beginning.

Rita Isn't that called jumpin' a sinkin' ship?

Frank So what? Do you really think there's any chance of us keeping it afloat?

She looks at him and then at the shelves

Rita *(seeing the empty whisky bottles)* 'Ey, Frank, if there was threepence back on each of those bottles you could buy Australia.

Frank *(smiling)* You're being evasive.

Rita *(going and sitting on a tea-chest)* I know. Tiger's asked me to go down to France with his mob.

Frank Will you?

Rita I dunno. He's a bit of a wanker really. But I've never been abroad. An' me mother's invited me to her's for Christmas.

Frank What are you going to do?

Rita I dunno. I might go to France. I might go to me mother's. I might even have a baby. I dunno. I'll make a decision, I'll choose. I dunno.

Frank has found a package hidden behind some of the books. He takes it down

Frank Whatever you do, you might as well take this ...

Rita What?

Frank *(handing it to her)* It's erm – well, it's er – it's a dress really. I bought it some time ago – for erm – for an educated woman friend – of mine ...

Rita takes the dress from the bag

I erm – don't – know if it fits, I was rather pissed when I bought it ...

to jump • to abandon **afloat** on the water **threepence back** *G.* 3 Pence Pfand **evasive** trying to avoid; *G.* ausweichend **mob** • group of friends **wanker** ['wæŋkə] masturbator; *here:* (a term of abuse) self-obsessed person **to fit** to be the correct size

Rita An educated woman, Frank? An' is this what you call a scholarly neckline?

Frank When choosing it I put on rather more emphasis on the word woman than the word educated.

Rita All I've ever done is take from you. I've never given anything.

Frank That's not true you've ...

Rita It is true. I never thought there was anythin' I could give you. But there is. Come here, Frank ...

Frank What?

Rita Come here ... *(She pulls out a chair)* Sit on that ...

Frank is bewildered

Sit ...

Frank sits and Rita, eventually finding a pair of scissors on the desk, waves them in the air

I'm gonna take ten years off you ...

She goes across to him and begins to cut his hair. As she gets close to his earlobe Frank cries out "Ouch"

Black-out

to take years off s.o. to make s.o. look younger

Anregungen, Vorschläge

EXPERIENCING A PLAY: SUGGESTIONS

The script as a 'potential play'

Unlike a short story or a novel, a play requires a performance to be complete. While the playwright provides the script – the 'raw material' in the form of dialogue and stage directions – it is the actors who breathe life into it. In other words, the medium of the play is both the script and the dramatization of the script.

This is not to say that you cannot appreciate a play until you have seen it performed on stage. When you read a play, as opposed to watching a performance, you look at it with fresh eyes. Your response will be unfiltered by the interpretations of the actors or the theatre director. It is your interpretation of the script – what you read into the lines and how you visualize the performance – that counts. You may need to rely on your imagination more than when you read a short story or novel, but think of this as an opportunity. The 'raw material' of the script is there for you to play with.

Reading with a purpose

To get the most out of reading a play, try to slip out of your role as a pupil studying it in class, and instead look at the script from the various points of view of the people who might be involved in a production of the play: the producer, the director, the actors, the stage manager, the set designer, and so on. Assign yourself their tasks.

- As a *producer,* you will need to assess the dramatic potential of the script. Is it good enough to be performed? What sort of audience would it appeal to?
- As a *director,* you will need to consider which themes to focus on, how the characters should be played, and how to interpret the stage directions. Where and how should the characters stand, sit or walk? What are the dramatic effects of off-stage noises or characters, and how can you make the most of them?
- As an *actor,* you will also think of how to portray the character you are playing. This requires careful study of not only your dialogue, but that of the other characters, too. The way you perceive

to assign to give s.th. to s.o. as their share of work

the character may be quite different from the way someone else does, so you will need to be able to defend your understanding of the character by referring to the text.

- As a *drama critic*, you will review the performance as a whole. Does it do justice to the script? How well do the actors portray the characters? Would you recommend the play to others?

Making sense of a script: Some useful hints

- Read the script aloud, with different manners of speaking for each character.
- Study the stage directions very carefully and draw a sketch of the stage set or sets.
- Try to visualise the characters on the set, i.e. where they are standing or sitting, or what they are doing.
- Study the characters in detail and try to work out what is typical of them, how they interact with each other, and whether they undergo any change during the course of the play.
- Pay close attention to pauses and silences. They are as revealing about the characters as the words they say.
- Watch out for themes or motifs the playwright may have planted at the beginning of the play. It is interesting to see how they are developed later in the play.
- Pause every now and then and ask yourself how the play might continue.
- Write scene summaries.
- Keep a journal in which you write down your feelings about and insights into the play.

Gunther Volk

revealing *here:* informative

ADDITIONAL MATERIAL

NON-FICTIONAL TEXTS

I. Lern Yerself Scouse. How to talk proper in Liverpool

Scouse – or to give it its full title, Lobscouse, is of course a type of food rather than a dialect; it is the native dish of the Liverpudlian, or Scouser. Scouse is to Liverpool what Bouillabaisse is to Marseilles or the Schnitzel to Vienna, but unlike many other dishes identified with their place of origin Scouse is derived not from a gourmandising love of food, but from sheer grinding poverty. It is a simple stew made from the cheapest cuts of meat, usually mutton, boiled with potatoes and onions. The meat, indeed, is optional; without it the stew becomes Blind Scouse. Either kind is eaten with red cabbage pickled in vinegar.
But somehow, the word does not look like an English one – in spite of the OED definitions of *lob* as "a lout clown, a hanging lump of flesh, or a country bumpkin". [...] To my great delight I discovered a clue, if not the answer, in a large, nearly a century old, German cookery book that had belonged to my mother:

Labskaus (Sailor's Dish, original recipe)
Boil a piece of fairly lean salt beef (or equal quantities of beef and ham) till soft and chop it into coarse pieces. Meanwhile, boil some potatoes in unsalted water and add a great quantity (!) of small onions, which have been braised in butter. Mash all this together, season with pepper and pour over it enough of the meat stock to produce a mash of soft consistency. This simple dish is extremely tasty and nourishing, especially when taken with pickled cucumber and a glass of beer *(Translation).*

There was clearly no poverty in *that* kitchen – and there is certainly no mention of a dish called Blindskaus. Another recipe for Labskaus appears in a German tourist leaflet written in a rather curious form

Liverpudlian • a person from Liverpool **to derive from** *G.* ableiten **to gourmandise** ['gʊəməndaɪz] to eat a lot and well **sheer** absolute **grinding poverty** *G.* bitterste Armut **stew** *G.* Eintopf **mutton** *G.* Hammelfleisch **optional** left to choice **to pickle** to preserve (in vinegar) **OED** Oxford English Dictionary **lout** clumsy, ill-mannered boy or man **bumpkin** clumsy or stupid country person **lean** without much fat **coarse** fairly large and irregular **to braise** to boil slowly in a closed dish **to season** *G.* würzen **stock** *G.* Suppenbrühe **nourishing** ['nʌrɪʃɪŋ] *G.* nahrhaft **cucumber** ['kjuːkʌmbə] *G.* Gurke

of English and differing from the recipe given above only in recommending that the gherkins be cooked in the stew, and a bayleaf added. Here the dish is claimed as "one of the classics among German sailors' fare". Brockhaus, the German Encyclopaedia Britannica, on the other hand, disclaims it and declares Labskaus to be "a Norwegian sailors' dish of salt beef or fish, with mashed potatoes". Other German dictionaries explain the words *Labe* as "refreshment, comfort" and *labberig* as "an insipid, soft food". We may, therefore, safely conclude that the origin of Lobscouse is to be found in some ship's galley on the high seas. [...]

There is, however, nothing insipid or soft about the Scouse that is spoken rather than eaten.

Here are a dozen expressions from Scouse which is spoken in the Liverpool area:

1. Ullo dur!
   Greetings; I am pleased to make your acquaintance.
2. La.
   I say, young man.
   Ere, tatty-ead!
   I say, young woman!
3. I don know a blind werd e says.
   I do not understand him.
   I wanna.
   I want to.
4. Give yer chin a rest.
   Please be silent.
5. She gorra mouf like a parish oven.
   She is rather talkative.
6. Yer gorra cob on.
   You are in a bad mood.
7. My feller.
   My husband.
   Im.
   My husband.
   (slightly derisive)
8. We wuz playin.
   We were playing.
9. I'll mug yer.
   I will pay for you.
   (mug is possibly short for money.
   mug: pieces of broken crockery used for money games)
10. I'm under de arm, doctor.
    I am feeling rather poorly, doctor.

gherkins ['gɜːkɪnz] pickled small cucumbers **bayleaf** *G.* Lorbeerblatt **fare** food **to disclaim** to refuse to have anything to do with **mashed potatoes** *G.* Kartoffelpüree **insipid** ▲ *G.* labberig **galley** ship's kitchen

(If the patient has lost his voice the doctor is expected to understand the appropriate gesture)

11. Let's run up de rattlers (dancers).
    Let us go upstairs.
12. She gorra face like a ruptured custard.
    She is not very attractive.

From: Shaw, Frank/Spiegel, Fritz/Kelly, Stan (eds.), Lern Yerself Scouse. How to talk proper in Liverpool. Volume One.
Liverpool: Scouse Press 1966, pp. 7–10.

2. John Honey, Does Accent Matter? The Pygmalion Factor

What reconciles me to the gradual and eventual passing of accent varieties in Britain is my awareness that accent differences are one of the greatest obstacles to genuine social equality in this country. So long as accents persist, they will be made the excuse for some people to discriminate against others and belittle them. It is no accident that the USA, where a much larger proportion of the population speak with a standard accent (General American) than is the case with RP in Britain, is plausibly regarded as a much more open and genuinely democratic society than our own. A similar judgement has been made on Australia, where nearly everybody speaks with the same accent, though in a varying degree of breath. [...] In helping children to come to terms with the fact that accents provide social information on which they will inevitably be judged, they must be given opportunities to listen to their own recorded voices on tape and helped to appraise the reactions of others to their voices, since it is well established that many – perhaps most – speakers with non-standard accents are unaware of how much their speech varies from the standard.

They should be told, too, that the *Pygmalion* story as recounted by Bernard Shaw is based on a crude over-simplification of the way accents can work in British society to transform people's social

to reconcile oneself to s.th. to reluctantly accept s.th. *G.* sich mit etwas aussöhnen **eventual** final **to persist** to (still) exist **to belittle** to make s.o. or s.th. seem unimportant **RP** (abbr.) Received Pronunciation **to appraise** to judge or assess the value of something **crude** primitive, simple

status. Making Eliza into a duchess (or her father into a Cabinet minister) as Shaw claimed was possible simply by changing their accents is nonsense. When people move into a completely different social circle they need to know not just how to speak acceptably but also what to say, and how to behave in accordance with the manners of the group. Nineteenth-century writers of books of etiquettes recognized this when they offered conversation material on topics in history, politics and even field sports, which a duchess would hear discussed around her in addition to social gossip. That Eliza would also need to know *what* to say was conceded by Shaw when he gave her her most famous line ("Not bloody likely!") the whole effect of which lies in its being uttered in a socially inappropriate setting. But even this detail is not authentic, since a genuine lapse into Cockney would have been much more likely to have produced "No bleedin' fear!"

Where Shaw was unquestionably right, however, was in calling urgent attention to language as a subject that deserves to be studied and, in both its written and spoken forms, taught more sympathetically to schoolchildren.

(London: Faber and Faber, 1989)

3. The Open University

From: Fact Sheets distributed by The Open University
Public Relations Department, Milton Keynes
Reproduced in this edition on the following pages.

etiquette formal rules of correct and polite behaviour **to concede** to admit s.th. is true

FACT SHEET NUMBER 1

An introduction to the University

ESTABLISHED by Royal Charter in 1969, the Open University has pioneered open and distance learning at university level in the United Kingdom. In just 25 years it has become Britain's largest single teaching institution.

In 1995 more than 150,000 students are registered with the Open University. In addition it is expected that some 51,000 self-contained study packs will be sold, many of which will be used by more than one person. Thus at least 210,000 people will be studying with the University in the current year.

HISTORY

The Open University was brought into existence by the grant of its Royal Charter in April 1969, but its origins go back much further than that.

Speculation about the use of radio for university-level education began as early as the 1920s, and the advent of television provided further impetus to such ideas, but none were realised. It was not until the early 1960s that firm proposals began to be developed. By then other countries, notably Canada, Australia, the USA and the Soviet Union were already engaged in distance teaching of various kinds.

In 1962 Michael Young (now Lord Young of Dartington), in an article in *Where* magazine, proposed 'an open university' to prepare people for the external degrees of London University. His own energies, however, went into the foundation of the National Extension College, and it was Harold Wilson (now Lord Wilson, then leader of the Opposition) who in a speech at Glasgow in 1963 launched the idea of a 'University of the Air' – a consortium of existing universities using broadcasting and correspondence tuition to bring their teaching to adult students in their own homes.

An independent university

At that time the idea attracted very little interest. It was never official Labour Party policy and remained very much Mr Wilson's personal project. After he became Prime Minister in 1964 he asked his Minister for the Arts, Jennie Lee (later Baroness Lee of Ashridge), to take responsibility for it.

Under Jennie Lee's leadership the concept emerged of an autonomous, independent university equal to any other. She overcame the scepticism and even hostility of the educational establishment by 'outsnobbing the snobs', as she put it herself: she brought together a Planning Committee which included five vice-chancellors, the principal of a polytechnic, and the leaders of two education authorities. Their recommendations eventually won the support of Jennie Lee's colleagues in the Cabinet, and the Open University at last became a reality.

In the early years the main priority was the creation of a viable undergraduate programme. The first 24,000 students were admitted in 1971. By the mid-70s there were more than 50,000 undergraduates and a wide range of courses for them to study.

Despite this rapid expansion the University was already planning its next step: a programme of 'continuing education' covering professional and scientific updating, social and community matters, and personal interest topics. Sir Peter Venables, who had chaired the original Planning Committee, returned to lead another committee which established the principles on which the resulting programmes of study have been based. During the 1980s this side of the University's work overtook the degree programme in student/client numbers.

HOW THE OU TEACHES

The characteristic feature of all Open University teaching is that it is at a distance – the courses come to the students in their own homes or, sometimes, places of work.

Courses are carefully designed to meet the needs of home-based students. At the heart of most courses are a series of specially-produced textbooks (known as 'units' within the OU). These are linked in most cases to other materials: radio and television programmes, audio and video tapes, home experiment kits and computer software.

Although students learn at home, there is plenty of support and human contact available. All registered students have a local tutor and counsellor, whom they can meet along with fellow students at one of the network of some 293 study centres throughout the UK. Elsewhere in Europe similar arrangements are being made where there are sufficient numbers of students.

Students also meet at the residential schools which are an integral part of many OU courses. Most undergraduate students attend at least one summer school, usually lasting a week; these are held on the campuses of other universities during their long vacation. Many management courses include weekend residential schools.

Open entry

No entry qualifications are required for Open University courses, other than for higher degrees. The only requirements are that applicants should be adults resident in the UK, or elsewhere in Europe. Limits of staffing and resources govern how many students can study a course each year, so there are sometimes quotas and waiting lists, but the basic principle is to accept anyone who genuinely wishes to study. In most years, however, applications for entry to the undergraduate programme outnumber the places available.

In its undergraduate admission policy in the UK the University strives to achieve a broad balance between numbers of students on arts/social sciences and maths/science/technology courses, and also tries to keep its student numbers in line with the distribution of population. Beyond these broad constraints, however, admission to the University is on a first-come first-served basis. Elsewhere in Europe, where full-cost fees are charged, it is simply a matter of responding to demand.

The amount of work expected of a student varies from course to course. A typical undergraduate course involves 12-14 hours study per week over a nine-month period. Open University Business School courses normally last for three or six months and a total of 110 hours or 220 hours study.

Some courses are presented in the form of self-contained study packs, suitable for individual or group study. Optional assessment may be available. Many large companies and public service bodies integrate these packs into their in-house training programmes.

PROGRAMMES OF STUDY

Undergraduate courses

The largest single group of OU students are those studying for a BA or BSc degree (more than 130,000 in 1995).

Students choose from a range of 130+ courses at first, second, third and fourth level, originated by eight faculties or schools: Arts, Social Sciences, Education, Health and Social Welfare, Management, Mathematics and Computing, Science and Technology.

Most courses are rated as worth 60 or 30 points in the Credit Accumulation & Transfer Scheme (CATS) widely used in UK higher education, according to the amount of work involved.

To gain a BA or BSc students must complete a minimum of 360 CATS points, equivalent to three years of full-time study. For an Honours degree 120 points must be at third or fourth level. Those who seek greater specialisation can continue up to a maximum of 480 CATS points. The assessment of students is rigorous, combining a number of assignments during the course and a three-hour invigilated examination. Both the continuous assessment and the exam count in the final course result. External assessors ensure that Open University standards are comparable with those of other British universities.

UK students pay tuition fees (£279 in 1995) and meet the costs of any residential school (£188 in 1995). They pay for their own books and travel. Students on courses with a substantial computing element need access to suitable personal computers. With stationery, travel and postage, the cost to an undergraduate of first year study, on a course which has a residential school, would be between £500 and £600. In subsequent years it might be less, as many higher level courses do not include a residential school. The total cost of a degree would be in the region of £2,700 (at 1995 prices), spread usually over four, five, or six years.

UK undergraduate fees do not represent the full economic cost of the courses; they are in effect subsidized by the University's grant from the Higher Education Funding Councils. OU students do not qualify for mandatory local authority grants. Some are helped by discretionary awards from local authorities or by their employers. Students who are unemployed or on a very low income may get help with their fees from a University fund.

Undergraduate and other courses are also available to people wishing to study without taking a degree. Study of this kind may be used for updating, refresher or general interest purposes.

Management courses

The Open University Business School is the largest provider of management training in the UK and has expanded into Europe. It offers a range of management training opportunities at different levels.

Short, practical courses for existing or newly-promoted managers are available to individuals, groups and organizations. For those who want to acquire a recognised qualification, taking a series of these courses can lead to a Professional Certificate or Professional Diploma in Management. The uppermost tier is a distance-taught MBA, for which either the Diploma or a good honours degree is the normal entry requirement.

Some 16,000 managers are taking Business School courses in 1995, including more than 5,000 registered for the MBA.

Other professional training

In manufacturing and computing the University offers two series of postgraduate courses designed to keep people abreast of the latest developments.

Course modules may be taken individually or as a route to a diploma or MSc degree.

For people working in education there are more than 100 courses and study packs to support professional development. Qualifications include certificates and diplomas, and an extremely popular MA in Education.

For those who want to enter teaching as a career, the University has a part-time Postgraduate Certificate in Education programme.

In the health and social welfare areas there is a wide range of options, from introductory study packs to courses leading to a diploma.

Personal and leisure interests

Study packs and short courses are available on topics such as parenthood, career development, personal health, the environment and the arts. Most are intended for use by people who wish to study on their own but some are linked to tutor packs to allow employers or community groups to set up study groups and training sessions.

Higher degrees

A major development for the University has been the programme of Master's degrees, achieved through a combination of course work and theses. The number of students has increased rapidly, from around 700 in 1987 to nearly 12,000 in 1995 – a figure equivalent to the total student population of many universities.

The University also offers opportunities to take research-based degrees of BPhil, MPhil and PhD, studied full- or part-time. There are 830 research students registered in 1995.

Modern languages

The latest major academic development is a programme of modern language courses. These are not introductory, but assume a basic level of competence. They are intended particularly for those who want to take their school-level language skills to a more advanced stage, whether for business or personal reasons.

The first French courses became available in 1995, and will be followed by German and Spanish.

EUROPE

Since 1992 the Open University has accepted students from all European Community countries – and, at its discretion, from other parts of Europe – into its undergraduate and other programmes of study. Courses are offered in English, and local support services are provided where student numbers permit. In 1995 there are more than 5,000 students in Western Europe.

There is also a particular demand from the former Soviet bloc for management training from the Open University Business School, which is already operating in Hungary, the Czech Republic, Slovakia, Romania, Bulgaria and Russia with courses translated into the indigenous languages. More than 8,000 students are taking OU courses in central and eastern Europe through these collaborative schemes.

Partnership arrangements in Singapore, Hong Kong and most recently the United Arab Emirates bring OU courses to another 11,000 people.

VALIDATION

In 1992 the University took on a new role, that of validating awards for a number of colleges and other institutions, as well as the degrees of independent postgraduate students.

This followed the winding up of the Council for National Academic Awards (CNAA), which had previously validated not only these awards but those of the former polytechnics. As the only university operating nationally, the OU was seen as a natural successor to the CNAA. It is also exploring new forms of validation, for example for the in-house training programmes of large companies.

In 1995 more than 7,000 students were taking OU-validated courses.

WHO ARE THE STUDENTS?

- The majority of Open University students are in their late twenties, thirties, or forties. The youngest are in their late teens, the oldest graduates (so far) in their nineties.
- Half of all OU students are women – the highest proportion of female students of any UK university.
- Three out of four undergraduate and associate students remain in paid employment throughout their studies, and are thus paying taxes and contributing to the national economy while also paying their own fees.
- Only one in five of those beginning their undergraduate studies have the minimum two A-levels necessary to enter other universities, while nearly half have no A-levels at all.
- About half of all OU undergraduates had fathers in 'blue collar' occupations, compared with about one-fifth at most other universities.
- The OU has always accepted a special responsibility to provide higher education for people with physical or sensory disabilities; currently some 4,500 of its students come into that category.
- Notwithstanding the open entry policy, about 80% of finally-registered undergraduates pass their first-year examinations and more than 55% successfully graduate four, five, six or more years later.

RESEARCH

Like all other universities, the OU regards research as a vital element in its activities. A healthy research programme helps to ensure that teaching at all levels is informed by the latest developments and that academic staff of the highest quality continue to be attracted to the University.

In the recent Research Assessment Exercise applied to all UK universities, the Open University received high ratings across a very broad range of subjects. Scores of 5 and 4 (representing work of international excellence) were awarded in educational technology, art and design, Earth sciences, geography, sociology, history of art, architecture and design, and education. Ratings of 3 (national excellence) went to psychology, biological sciences, statistics, computer science, general engineering, politics, international studies, social policy, English language and literature, philosophy and music.

FUNDING

In 1993 the Open University became part of the newly-integrated funding arrangements for higher education in the UK. It will in future receive its core grants from the Higher Education Funding Council for England, although because of its UK-wide operations it is also eligible (uniquely) to receive funds from the Councils for Wales, Scotland, and Northern Ireland. Prior to this, the University had been funded by block grant direct from the Department for Education.

The University's financial year runs from August-July.

The HEFCE block grant in 1993/4 (£104 million) represented 57.7% of the University's total operating budget of £180.4m. Fee income from students totalled 32.6% (£58.8m) and other income 3.6% (£6.5m)

For the 1994-5 financial year the HEFCE has announced grants in the region of £104m for the Open University. This includes £11m for research.

Cost-effectiveness

The cost structure of the Open University is very different from those of most other universities. Developing its complex, multi-media courses is expensive – but they can then be taught to many thousands of students over a period of years. Because the OU does not need lecture theatres, laboratories or halls of residence, it can expand its student numbers at very low marginal costs.

GOVERNMENT STRUCTURE

The Open University is governed by two bodies, Council and Senate. The Council is responsible for financial and employment decisions, while the Senate has authority for academic matters.

A number of major committees form the next tier of the government structure: these include the Academic Board, which acts as the executive for Senate, and the Strategic Planning and Resources Committee and Operational Planning and Budget Committee which report both to Council and Senate.

Members of the University Council represent a range of interests and are appointed by, among others, the Privy Council, the Committee of Vice-Chancellors and Principals, local education authorities, the BBC, the University Senate, and the students' and graduates' associations.

All full-time academic staff of the University are members of Senate, which also has representation for tutorial and counselling staff, administrative and secretarial staff and for students and graduates.

Officers and departments

The chief executive of the University is the Vice-Chancellor. He is assisted by a senior management team of five Pro-Vice-Chancellors, whose areas of responsibility are currently as follows: Strategy and Planning; Student, Tutorial and Regional Services; Curriculum Development; Technology Development; Quality Assurance and Research.

The University's administration is headed by the University Secretary. Administration in the Open University is on a large scale, appropriate to the number of its students and the wide range of its activities. Among the main divisions are student administration, academic administration, finance, management services, and estates.

Another major area of the University is known as Operations: this includes publishing, graphic design, warehousing and distribution services. It is headed by a director.

The University has 13 regional centres in the UK, each with a director and a staff of academics and administrators. Their role is largely the admission, tuition and counselling of students: they appoint and supervise some 7,300 part-time tutors and counsellors, arrange tutorials, and work with central colleagues on the complex organization of residential schools and examinations.

The full-time staff of the University totals just over 3,500, of whom 800 are academic, 700 administrators, and 1,200 secretarial and clerical.

This Fact Sheet is one of a series describing various aspects of the Open University, produced by:

Public Relations Department
The Open University
Walton Hall, Milton Keynes MK7 6AA
Telephone 01908 274066 Fax 01908 652247 LH:JM/795

EUROPEAN FACT SHEET 4

The Open University in Germany

THE OU IN EUROPE

THE Open University is open to all adults aged 18 or over resident in the United Kingdom and throughout the European Union, and in various other European countries.

There are no entry qualifications for most OU courses and study programmes, including the BA/BSc degree programme. All courses are taught in English.

THE OU IN GERMANY

- The Open University has been present in Germany since 1992.
- There are study centres at Neuss, Frankfurt, Hamburg and Munich.
- The OU and the University of Hamburg are collaborating on a joint research project under the "Socrates" scheme to investigate the use of OU courses and materials.

Courses

- Distribution of courses between faculties:

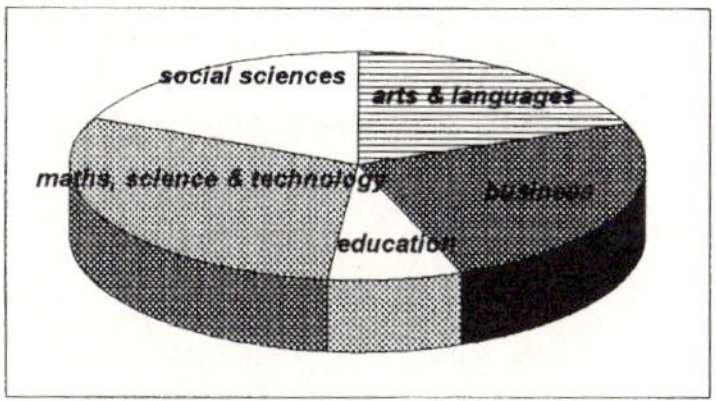

- The most popular 1996 post-Level 1 undergraduate courses are "Introduction to Psychology" and "The Enlightenment".
- 21 tutorial and counselling staff are employed in Germany.

Who are the students?

- In 1996, 500 people in Germany are studying with the OU.
- 70% of students work full time while completing their courses.
- Level of qualifications at entry to the OU:

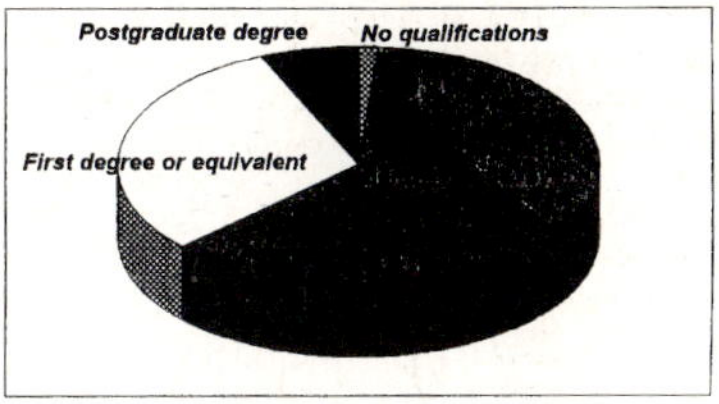

- Around 1 in 4 students speak English as their second language.
- 47% of students are male, compared to the European average of 56%.
- 33% of students have some level of professional qualification.

For more information on the Open University in Germany, please contact:

Louise Henrichsen
Open University (North West Germany)
Postfach 101360
40833 Ratingen

Tel: *(02102) 87 1814*
Fax: *(02102) 87 1864*
Email: *L.Henrichsen@open.ac.uk*

Matthew Hawkes
Open University (South Germany)
Postfach 62
85256 Vierkirchen

Tel: *(08139) 7373*
Fax: *(08139) 7365*
Email: *M.Hawkes@open.ac.uk*

Marion Bruhn-Suhr
The Open University
(North Germany and New Länder)
Universität Hamburg (Arbeitsstelle für wissenschaftliche Weiterbildung)
Vogt Kölln-Strasse 30
Haus E
22527 Hamburg

Tel: *(040) 5494 2478*
Fax: *(040) 5494 2652*
Email: *aww@aww.uni-hamburg.de*

Royal Charter written statement by a ruler or government granting certain rights and/or privileges to a town, company, university etc. signed by the ruling king or queen **to pioneer** to be the first to do s.th. **self-contained study packs** packets of books, leaflets etc. which contain all the material necessary to complete a particular course **to grant** to agree to give or allow s.th. **advent** ['ædvənt] beginning or arrival **impetus** force which keeps s.th. moving **to be engaged in** to be involved in/with s.th. **to launch** to start **tuition** teaching **eventually** in the end **viable** practical *G.* realisierbar **to overtake** *here:* to become greater than **to meet the needs of** to provide everything that is required of s.o. or s.th. **kit** pack containing equipment needed to carry out an activity **residential school** a course involving going to stay somewhere else; also: any school where one lives while one studies **to staff** to provide the personnel required to carry out the task **to govern** to determine, to control **to strive** to try hard **in line with** corresponding to *G.* entsprechend **constraints** rules or circumstances which limit what one can do **to respond to demand** to act according to the number of people who want to have or use a certain product **optional** voluntary **assessment** evaluation or opinion *G.* Benotung **public service bodies** organisations or companies which provide essential services, e.g. water, electricity, telecommunications **BA** (abbr.) Bachelor of Arts degree (geisteswissenschaftlicher Hochschulabschluss) **BSc** (abbr.) Bachelor of Science degree (naturwissenschaftlicher Hochschulabschluss) **130+** more than 130 **are rated as worth 60 or 30 points** are considered to have a value of 60 or 30 points in the CATS scheme (see below) **Credit Accumulation & Transfer Scheme (CATS)** a system used by universities where courses are given a certain amount of points so that if s.o. changes university before they finish their degree the courses taken at the old university will be recognised by the new university **honours degree** a degree with a grade *G.* ein benoteter Hochschulabschluss, d.h. ein *degree* ohne *honours* hat keine Note – außer „bestanden“ **assignment** work (usually an essay or project) done by the student at home **invigilated examination** an examination where an invigilator (supervisor) is present to make sure the rules of the examination are not broken **stationery** writing materials *e.g.* pens, paper **Funding Councils** government bodies which provide money for universities and schools **mandatory grant** a grant (*G.* Stipendium) given by a Local Education Authority (LEA) to a student in higher education according to a certain set of rules set by the government **discretionary grant** sometimes a grant is given to a student who is not eligible for a mandatory grant (for instance if he/she has already had one) according the LEA's discretion. The LEA can give a discretionary grant to any student they think deserves it, according to the circumstances **fund** a collection of money **to update** *here:* referring to those people who have studied in the past and wish to know what the latest thinking is **uppermost tier** highest level **MBA** (abbr.) Master of Business Administration degree – a degree for people who wish to go into business management **to keep abreast of** to make people aware of what is happening in a certain area of study or thinking **modules** ['mɒdju:lz] parts of a course which are self-contained. Some degrees are modular, that is to say they are split up into self-contained units or modules – as opposed to linear (where each course follows the previous one). Each student must complete a certain number of modules to complete the degree (similar to the German system) **MSc degree** (abbr.) Master of Science degree **parenthood** being parents/a parent **training sessions** periods of time spent learning **BPhil, MPhil, PhD** (abbr.) Bachelor of Philosophy, Master of Philosophy, Doctor of Philosophy – degrees consisting of research and writing a dissertation **to assume a basic level of competence** to expect a small amount of knowledge from the student **at somebody's discretion** *G.* nach jmds. Ermessen **indigenous** [ɪn'dɪdʒɪnəs] belonging to a particular country or area **collaborative schemes** arrangements where different countries or organisations work together toward mutual goals **validation** the act of making s.th. legally effective or usable or valid **to wind (s.th) up** *here: to* bring to an end **blue-collar** referring to industry and manual work (as opposed to business or office work which is white-collar) **sensory** referring to sight and hearing **notwithstanding** *G.* ungeachtet

„Universität der zweiten Chance“ erobert Europa

Von RALPH FLEISCHHAUER

Hobby oder berufliche Weiterbildung – rund 210 000 Menschen studieren an der britischen Open University

Die Zeiten sind unsicher geworden. Viele Menschen fürchten um ihre Arbeitsplätze, junge Leute wachsen oft ohne sichere Zukunftsaussichten heran. Dass das Klima auf dem Arbeitsmarkt immer rauer wird, haben die Arbeitnehmer in vielen anderen Ländern früher zu spüren bekommen als in Deutschland. So beispielsweise in Großbritannien. Im Wettbewerb um Arbeitsplätze wird die eigene Ausbildung immer wichtiger. Kein Wunder, dass berufsbegleitende Studien für viele Briten eine Selbstverständlichkeit geworden sind. Die „Open University“, die größte Fernuniversität Europas, spielt dabei eine wichtige Rolle. Auch auf dem europäischen Festland werden nun ihre Kurse angeboten.

„Harold Wilsons beste Idee“, nennt Andrew Robinson die Open University. Diese Fernuniversität sei das Lieblingskind des ehemaligen Regierungschefs der Labour-Party gewesen, meint der Leiter des Regionalzentrums in Newcastle. Die „Universität der zweiten Chance“ sollte allen Briten auch nach ihrer Schulzeit noch eine Möglichkeit bieten, ihre beruflichen Perspektiven zu verbessern. Und als die Open University 1969 aus der Taufe gehoben wurde, waren Fernsehen und Radio wichtige Paten. Bis heute ist die Rundfunkanstalt BBC an der Entwicklung der Kurse beteiligt, übernimmt sie die Produktion von Fernseh- und Radiosendungen, von Video- und Audio-Kassetten.

Rund 210 000 Personen belegten im vergangenen Jahr Kurse an dieser größten Fernuniversität Europas. Das Durchschnittsalter der Studenten liegt bei 37 Jahren. Die Kurse der Open University sind offen für jedermann, also auch für jene, die keinen Schulabschluss besitzen, der an anderen Universitäten zu einem Studium berechtigen würde.

Staatliche Unterstützung

In Milton Keynes, einer neuen, 180 000 Einwohner zählenden Stadt im Nordwesten Londons, hat die Hochschule ihren Hauptsitz. Der „studentenfreie Campus“ umfasst mehrere Institute, Bibliotheken, Geschäfte, ein BBC-Gebäude und Wohnbereiche für die Mitarbeiter – allein in Milton Keynes sind es 2500 – darunter 500 Dozenten und 228 BBC-Angestellte. Insgesamt sind bei der Open University mit ihren 13 Regionalzentren in Großbritannien 3500 Personen hauptamtlich beschäftigt. Rund 200 Millionen britische Pfund (ca. 460 Millionen Mark) betrug der Etat im vergangenen Jahr. 58 Prozent der Mittel kommen vom Staat, der Rest wird über Studiengebühren eingenommen.

Offener Zugang

Der liberale Umgang der Briten mit der Tatsache, dass diese Hochschule jedermann offen steht, ist bemerkenswert; zumindest aus deutscher Sicht. Tut man sich hierzulande doch äußerst schwer damit, die Hochschulen für erfolgreiche Berufstätige zu öffnen, wenn diese kein Abitur haben. Das Meister-Studium ist da allenfalls ein Anfang.

Die „Offenheit“ der Open University unterscheidet sie denn auch grundsätzlich von einer Fernuniversität wie der in Hagen. Hinzu kommt, dass Hagen ein weitaus geringeres Fächerangebot hat, man also dort keineswegs all das studieren kann, was eine Volluniversität anbietet. Der Nachteil dieser Offenheit ist jedoch, dass es einige Zeit dauert, bis alle Studenten etwa den gleichen Stand erreicht haben. Einjährige Grundlagenkurse dienen deshalb dazu, die Eingangsvoraussetzungen anzugleichen.

Ob ein Studienabschluss allerdings gut angesehen ist, zeigt sich erst auf dem Arbeitsmarkt. In England gibt es mit der Anerkennung der Open-University-Abschlüsse keine Probleme. Das bestätigt Susan Gane vom Londoner Bildungsministerium ausdrücklich „Die Open University ist eine Hochschule wie viele andere auch, ihre Absolventen haben auf dem Arbeitsmarkt die gleichen Chancen.“

„Das Studium an der Open University ist kein Zuckerschlecken“, meint Geoffrey Peters, der in Milton Keynes für die Planung zuständig ist. Durchschnittlich 15 bis 20 Stunden müssten die Studenten pro Woche in die Kurse investieren, und da drei Viertel von ihnen gleichzeitig im Beruf stünden, sei das für sie schon eine arge Belastung. Trotzdem sei die Abbrecherquote an der Open University relativ gering. Ein Grund dafür sei die gute Betreuung der Kunden, meint Peters.

In Großbritannien kümmern sich rund 7000 Tutoren um die Studenten, stehen ihnen bei Studienproblemen hilfreich zur Seite, bieten Treffen an, die das Heimstudium ergänzen. Die Tutoren sind oftmals Frauen, die ihre akademische Laufbahn wegen der Familie beendet haben, aber noch ein berufliches Betätigungsfeld suchen.

Einmal im Jahr treffen sich die Studenten zu sogenannten „Summer Schools“. Bei diesen meist einwöchigen Treffen wird das Gelände traditioneller Hochschulen genutzt, die dann Semesterferien haben. Hier kommen Studenten der einzelnen Fachrichtungen zu einem gemeinsamen Seminar zusammen.

Stolz verweist Annette Mathias, Pressesprecherin der Open University, auf die Tatsache, dass jeder vierte Brite jemanden kennt, der an einem oder mehreren Kursen teilgenommen hat. „Die Open University ist eine der größten Erfolgsgeschichten dieses Jahrhunderts", meint sie.

Minister als Kunden

Zu den Studenten der Fernuniversität gehören Hausfrauen ebenso wie Minister. „Das gesamte äthiopische Kabinett, einschließlich Regierungschef Meles Zenawi, hat bei uns studiert", erzählt Tony Stapleton von der Open University Business School, die sich um die Management-Schulung kümmert. Nachdem die Rebellen 1991 die Mengistu-Diktatur gestürzt hatten, hätten sie sich so für die schwierige Aufgabe der Regierungsgeschäfte fortgebildet – erfolgreich im Übrigen, meint der Hochschullehrer.

Doch alle Erfolge können nicht darüber hinwegtäuschen, dass auch die Open University unter der Finanzknappheit der öffentlichen Kassen leidet. Die staatlichen Zuschüsse stagnieren, während die Kosten steigen. Neue Medien wie der Computer und seine Einsatzmöglichkeiten in internationalen Datennetzen bieten zwar die besten Zukunftsperspektiven für Fernstudien – doch sie verschlingen auch große Summen. „Expansion" heißt daher das Zauberwort.

„Wir müssen unsere Kurse im Ausland besser verkaufen", meint Roger Penfound von der BBC. „Die Entwicklungskosten sind dieselben, ob ein Kurs nun von 5000 oder 10 000 Leuten belegt und bezahlt wird." Nicht zuletzt deshalb will die Open University ihre Aktivitäten im englischsprachigen Ausland, aber auch auf dem europäischen Festland verstärken.

Rund 6000 Studenten zählt die Fernuniversität derzeit in den westeuropäischen Ländern, 600 davon leben in Deutschland. Angefangen hat die Hochschule 1992 mit ein paar Angehörigen der britischen Armee in den Benelux-Staaten. Heute unterhält sie mehrere Studienzentren in Europa, darunter eines in Neuss. Mit zahlreichen Universitäten existieren Partnerschaftsverträge; dort kann man sich über das Angebot der Open University informieren. Natürlich ist das Netz der Tutoren auf dem europäischen Festland nicht annähernd so dicht wie in England, doch glaubt Liz Manning, dass dies angesichts der neuen Medien kein großer Nachteil sein muss. Die ehemalige Tutorin ist zuständig für die deutschen und österreichischen Studenten. Sie sitzt im Regionalzentrum Newcastle, von wo aus die europäischen Aktivitäten der Hochschule koordiniert werden.

Export-Schlager

„Auf dem Festland ist besonders das Interesse an unseren Management-Kursen groß", berichtet Liz Manning. Wie Andrew Robinson ist sie davon überzeugt, dass speziell diese Ausbildung ein Export-Schlager werden wird. Da die Kurse der Business School nicht staatlich subventioniert werden, liegen die Gebühren allerdings deutlich höher als bei den anderen Studienangeboten. In England werden solche Kurse häufig von den Unternehmen bezahlt, die ein großes Interesse daran haben, dass sich ihre Angestellten privat – und damit in ihrer Freizeit – fortbilden. Schließlich kommt das neue Know-how auch den Firmen zugute. Und deshalb – davon sind die Mitarbeiter in Newcastle überzeugt – wird sich dieses Angebot auch auf dem europäischen Festland durchsetzen.

Daten und Fakten zur Open University

Geistes-, Sozial-, Natur- und Umweltwissenschaften, Mathematik und Technologie – in diesen Bereichen bietet die Open University Kurse an, mit denen der Bachelor, der unterste akademische Grad des britischen Bildungssystems, erworben werden kann. Rund 1000 bis 1600 Mark kosten die zum Bachelor führenden Kurse pro Jahr in Deutschland. Allerdings zieht sich ein solches Studium über fünf und mehr Jahre hin. In den Gebühren sind sämtliche Studienmaterialien, wie Bücher, Video- und Audio-Kassetten enthalten, nicht allerdings die Reisekosten für die meist einwöchigen Summer-Schools.

Ein Sonderfall ist die Open University Business-School (OUBS). Sie bietet Management-Kurse an, für die ein Einstiegsalter von 27 Jahren sowie Berufserfahrung Voraussetzung sind. Diese Studiengänge schließen mit dem Master of Business Administration ab, einem Abschluss, der nach frühestens drei Jahren erreicht werden kann, wenn der Kursteilnehmer bereits ein abgeschlossenes Studium vorweisen kann. Ist dies nicht der Fall, verlängert sich der Kurs um mindestens ein Jahr. Da diese Kurse nicht staatlich subventioniert werden, liegen die Gebühren deutlich höher: Zwischen 3600 und 6800 Mark werden pro Jahr fällig.

Für alle Kurse gilt: Gute Englischkenntnisse sind Voraussetzung.

Nähere Informationen erteilt: Louise Henrichsen, Open University, Postfach 101360 in 40833 Ratingen, Telefon 0 21 02 / 87 18 14 (Fax: 0 21 02 / 87 18 64)

Rheinische Post, 6. Juni 1996

4. Willy Russell, Educating the Author

I was born in Whiston, which is just outside Liverpool. They talk funny in Whiston. To a Liverpudlian everyone else talks funny. Fortunately, when I was five my mum and dad moved to Knowsley, onto an estate full of Liverpudlians who taught me how to talk correctly.

My dad worked in a factory (later, having come to hate factory life, he got out and bought a chip shop) and my mother worked in a warehouse; in those days there was a common ritual called employment. I went to school just down the road from my grandma's mobile grocers (it was in an old charabanc which had long since lost any chance of going anywhere, but everyone called it the mobile).

In school I learned how to read very early. Apart from reading books I played football and kick-the-can and quite enjoyed the twice-weekly gardening lessons. We each had a plot, and at the end of the summer term we could take home our turnips and lettuces and radish and stuff. We used to eat it on the way. Our headmaster (Pop Chandler) had a war wound in his leg, and everyone said it was "'cause of the shrapnel". When we went to the baths (if he was in a good mood) he'd show us this hole in his leg. It was horrible. It was blue. We loved looking at it.

Other than reading books, gardening, playing football and looking at shrapnel wounds I didn't care much for school. I watched the telly a lot. Never went to any theatres or anything like that. Saw a show at the village hall once but it was all false. They talked funny and got married at the end. I only remember it 'cause I won the raffle, a box of fruit, with a coconut right in the middle. When we opened it the coconut stunk. It was bad.

When I was eleven they sent me to a secondary school in Huyton. Like all the other Knowsley kids I was frightened of Huyton. There were millions of new houses there and flats, and everyone said there

estate area of land developed for residential purposes, with the houses built on it **to get out** • to leave hastily **warehouse** *G.* Lagerhaus **charabanc** [ˈʃærəbæŋ] a large excursion bus with seats facing forward **kick-the-can** an outdoor game, similar to 'hide and seek' where a can is put in a central place guarded by one person. The game is won when a member of the group succeeds in kicking the can unobserved by the person looking for the rest of the group **plot** a section of land **turnip** *G.* Steckrübe **lettuce** *G.* Kopfsalat **radish** [ˈrædɪʃ] *G.* Rettich, *hier:* Radieschen **stuff** • *G. hier:* so etwas **shrapnel** (small pieces of metal from) an explosive shell or bomb **other than** apart from **to care for** to like; to enjoy **telly** • television **raffle** a lottery in which numbered tickets are sold to a large number of people, the holder of a ticket selected at random wins a prize

were gangs with bike chains and broken bottles and truck spanners. What everyone said was right; playtime had nothing to do with play, it was about survival. Thugs roamed the concrete and casually destroyed anything that couldn't move fast enough. Dinner time was the same only four times as long.

If you were lucky enough to survive the food itself you then had to get out into the playground world of protection rackets, tobacco hustlers, trainee contract killers and plain no-nonsense sadists. And that's without the teachers!

"Anders" his name was, the metalwork teacher. All the other kids loved metalwork. First thing we had to do was file a small rectangle of metal so that all the sides were straight; this would then be name-stamped and used as a nameplate to identify each kid's work. I never completed mine. After a matter of weeks other kids had moved from making nameplates to producing anything from guns and daggers to boiler-room engines, whilst it was obvious that I was never going to be able to get the sides of my piece of metal straight. Eventually it was just a sliver, a near perfect needle, though not straight. I showed it to him, Anders; I couldn't hide it from him any longer. He chucked it in the bin and wordlessly handed me another chunk of metal and indicated that I had to do it again and again and again until I did it *right*! And I did, for a whole school year, every metal-work lesson, tried and failed and with every failure there came a chunk of metal and the instruction to do it again. I started to have terrible nightmares about Anders. It's the only time I can remember feeling real hatred for another human being.

After another year I moved schools, to Rainford where it used to be countryside, where they all talked funny, where the thugs were rather old-fashioned, charming even. Whereas in Huyton you could be bike-chained to bits without warning, in Rainford the thugs observed some sort of manners: "Ey you, does t' want t' fight wi me?" You could still get hurt, of course, and some of the teachers were headcases, but there were no sadists; metalwork was not on the curriculum; there were fields and lawns in place of concrete play-

truck lorry *(especially AE.)* **spanner** *G.* Schraubenschlüssel **thug** a person who uses violence or brutality **to roam** to wander about with no particular goal **concrete** *G.* Beton **casually** *G.* beiläufig **protection racket** *G.* Erpresserorganisation **hustler** • *G.* Schwindler **trainee** [treiˈniː] person who is being trained **contract** *G.* Vertrag **sadist** person who gets pleasure from cruelty to others **dagger** *G.* Dolch **sliver** [ˈslɪvə] a very thin piece **to chuck** • *G.* schmeißen **chunk** a short thick piece **headcase** a person not mentally stable **curriculum** *G.* Lehrplan

Willy Russell

grounds and compared to Huyton it was paradise. We even had a long lesson every week called "silent reading"; just enter the classroom and pick up a book, start reading and as long as you made no noise you were left completely alone with your book. I remember clearly, during one of these lessons, locked into a novel, the sun streaming through the windows, experiencing the feeling of total peace and security and thinking what a great thing it must be to write books and create in people the sort of feeling the author had created in me.

I wanted to be a writer!

It was a wonderful and terrible thought – wonderful because I sensed, I knew, it was the only thing for me. Terrible because how could I, a kid from the "D" stream, a piece of factory fodder, ever change the course that my life was already set upon? How the hell could I ever be the sort of person who could become a writer? It was a shocking and ludicrous thought, one that I hid deep in myself for years, but one that would not go away.

stream in schools one of the classes into which children of the same age are divided according to ability **'D' stream** the lowest stream **fodder** food for farm animals **factory fodder** ordinary factory workers; cf cannonfodder: *G.* Kanonenfutter **ludicrous** ['lu:dɪkrəs] absurd

During my last year at school they took us to a bottle-making factory in St. Helens, me and all the other kids who were obviously factory types. I could feel the brutality of the place even before I entered its windowless walls. Inside the din and the smell was overpowering. Human beings worked in there but the figures I saw, feeding huge and relentlessly hungry machines seemed not to be a part of humanity but a part of the machinery itself. Those men who were fortunate enough to not have to work directly with the machinery, the supervisors, foremen I suppose, glared, prodded, occasionally shouted. Each one of them looked like Anders from the metalwork class.

Most of the kids with whom I visited that place accepted that it was their lot to end up in there. Some even talked of the money they would earn and made out that they couldn't wait to get inside those walls.

But, in truth, I think they all dreaded it as much as I. Back in school I stared at the geography books I hadn't read, the history pages and science I hadn't studied, the maths books (which would still be a mystery today, even if I'd studied them from birth), and I realised that with only six months schooling to go, I'd left it all hopelessly too late. Like it or not I'd end up in a factory. There was no point in trying to catch up with years of schoolwork in a mere six months.

And so I didn't. The months I had left were spent sagging school and going to a dark underground club every lunchtime. It was called the Cavern, and the smell of sweat in there was as pungent as any in a factory, the din was louder than any made by machines. But the sweat was mingled with cheap perfume and was produced by dancing; and the noise was music, made by a group called the Beatles.

One afternoon in summer I left the Cavern after the lunchtime session and had to go to the Bluecoat Chambers to sit an examination, the result of which would determine how suited I was to become an apprentice printer. I didn't want to be an apprentice printer; I wanted to be back in the Cavern. I did the exam because my dad thought it would be a good thing. I answered the questions on how many men it would take to lift three tons of coal in seven hours if it took one man two minutes to lift a sack of coal on a rainy day etc. And I wrote the essay of my choice (titled: A Group Called The Beatles). And I failed.

din • deafening noise **overpowering** *G.* überwältigend **relentlessly** *G.* unaufhörlich **supervisor** person in charge; *G.* Aufseher **foreman** *G.* Vorarbeiter **to glare** to stare fiercely **to prod** *G.* antreiben **lot** fate; *G.* Schicksal **to make out** to pretend **to sag school** • to stay away from school without permission **pungent** sharp and piercing **to mingle with** to mix with **apprentice** *G.* Lehrling; Azubi

At home there were conferences, discussions, rows and slanging matches all on the same subject – me and the job I'd get. Eventually my mother resolved it all. She suggested I become a ladies' hairdresser! I can only think that a desire to have her hair done free must have clouded her normally reasonable mind. It was such a bizarre suggestion that I went along with it. I went to a college for a year or so and pretended to learn all about hairdressing. In reality most of my time was spent at parties or arranging parties. It was a good year but when it ended I had to go to work. Someone was actually prepared to hire me as a hairdresser, to let me loose on the heads of innocent and unsuspecting customers. There were heads scalded during shampooing, heads which should have become blond but turned out green, heads of Afro-frizz (before Afro-frizz had been invented) and heads rendered temporarily bald. Somehow, probably from moving from one shop to another before my legendary abilities were known, I survived. For six years I did a job I didn't understand and didn't like. Eventually I even had my own small salon and it was there that on slack days I would retire to the back room and try to do the one and only thing I felt I understood, and felt I could do: write.

I wrote songs mostly but tried, as well, to write sketches and poetry, even a book. But I kept getting interrupted by women who, reasonably enough on their part, wanted their hair done. It dawned upon me that if ever I was to become a writer I had first to get myself into the sort of world which allowed for, possibly even encouraged, such aspiration. But that would mean a drastic change of course. Could I do it? Could I do something which those around me didn't understand? I would have to break away. People would be puzzled and hurt. I compromised. I sensed that the world in which I would be able to write would be the academic world. Students have long holidays. I'd be able to spend a good part of the year writing and the other part learning to do a job, teaching perhaps, which would pay the rent. I wasn't qualified to train as a teacher but I decided to dip my toe in the water and test the temperature. I enrolled in a night

row [raʊ] *G.* Krach **slanging match** a verbal confrontation using abusive language **to resolve** to find a solution to (a question or problem) **to go along with** to agree to **unsuspecting** *G.* ahnungslos **to scald s.o.** [skɔːld] to burn s.o. with very hot water **frizz** close mass of short curls **to render** to make **bald** [bɔːld] without hair **slack** with little work **to retire to** to go away (to some place) **sketch** brief story, account or description; short (usually one-scene) comedy, often musical **to dawn on** (or **upon**) to become suddenly clear to **aspiration** ambition **to break away from** to separate from **to dip** *G.* eintauchen **to enrol** *G.* sich einschreiben

class for "O" Level English Literature and passed it. To go to a college though I'd need at least five "O" Levels. Taking them at night school would take too long. I had to find a college which would let me take a full-time course, pack everything into one year. I found a college but no authority was prepared to give me a maintenance grant or even pay my fees. I knew I couldn't let the course go, knew I could survive from day to day, but how was I going to find the money to pay the fees? The hairdressing paid nothing worth talking of.

I heard of a job, a contract job in Fords, cleaning oil from the girders high above the machinery. With no safety equipment whatsoever and with oil on every girder the danger was obvious. But the money was big.

I packed up the hairdresser's and joined the night-shift girder cleaners. Some of them fell and were injured, some of them took one look at the job and walked away. Eventually there were just a few of us desperate or daft enough to take a chance.

I stayed in that factory just long enough to earn the fees I needed, no extras, nothing. Once I'd earned enough for the fees I came down from the girders, collected my money and walked away. I enrolled at the college and one day in September made my way along the stone-walled drive. The obvious difference in age between me and the sixteen-year-olds pouring down the drive made me feel exposed and nervous but, as I entered the glass doors of Childwall College, I felt as if I'd made it back to the beginning. I could start again. I felt at home.

Sept. 1983

maintenance grant *G.* Unterhaltszuschuss **fees** money paid every term to a college/university by the students **girder** *G.* Tragbalken **to pack up** • to leave hastily and unceremoniously **daft** foolish; crazy

5. Educating Lisa

YOU ONLY GET ONE CHANCE – AND I'M NOT WASTING IT
By Barbara Jones

The best of Britain's well-bred young brains start a new term at Oxford University tomorrow, more than half of them from top public schools.

One brilliant exception is 25-year-old Lisa Connerty.

She has arrived from Toxteth, the toughest part of Liverpool, with her two small children and several plastic bags full of clothes and toys. For this single parent who rolls her own cigarettes, *Educating Rita* is about to become *Educating Lisa.*

Unlike Rita in the Oscar-winning film, Lisa hasn't just struggled her way on to an Open University course. She has broken out of a city slum and won a place at Worcester College, reading English.

BABIES

'I can't quite believe I'm here,' she said. 'I'm going to work like mad to see if I can get myself a First.'

She added at her university flat where toys cluttered the little hall: 'One don kept asking how I was going to do all this and look after my children. They forget I've brought them up on my own for years already.'

Lisa, a barmaid's daughter, left school when she was 16, and had two babies by the time she was 19. Then her marriage went wrong and she found herself alone with her two daughters, Melita, now seven, and Naomi, five.

She spent her days drinking coffee with other bored mums until she remembered how, as a child, she read Jane Austen and Henry James from her grandmother's bookshelves. She trekked to the public library to do it again.

She moved into Toxteth with a girlfriend and they shared baby-sitting while Lisa swotted for nine months to get her three A-levels at the local college of further education. There her teacher told her: 'Don't just try for university. Try for Oxford.'

As she took her place in the grand college dining hall she said: 'There's a lot of rich kids at Oxford who'll spend their time here throwing bread rolls at each other. But you only get one chance at a place like this and I'm not going to waste mine.'

The Mail on Sunday,
October 12, 1986

well-bred from a "good" family **a First** the top mark in a British degree **don** old-fashioned term for a teacher at a university, esp. Oxford or Cambridge **Jane Austen** English novelist (1775-1817), wrote *Pride and Prejudice, Sense and Sensibility, Emma* etc. **Henry James** American novelist (1843-1916) who lived in England, wrote *The Turn of the Screw, The Ambassadors* etc. **to swot** • to study very hard *G.* büffeln

6. Folk Tale from Liverpool

PLAYS AND PLAYERS

JOHN BARBER meets a writer with the working-class audience at heart

I was apprehensive about meeting Willy Russell from Liverpool. I expected a hairy-chested macho, militantly working-class, all beard and cloth cap. There was no knowing what he might do with his hobnail boots if he'd read my opinion of his musical "Blood Brothers". I just hoped he knew I'd championed his play about the Beatles, and admired his "Educating Rita".

Tall, slim, young for 36, the man was certainly bearded but as gentle and civilised as Jeremy Irons, his voice only as northern as his light sounding of the "t" in often. I've never met a friendlier chap, and few as interesting. Not since Brendan Behan has a proletarian writer found so big an audience.

"Alternative theatre" in basements seating 80 are not for Willy Russell. He wants to reach "that massive untapped audience ignored by theatre for 150 years". It cost him dear: his rise hurt a lot of people close to him. He left school at 15 and for six years worked as (he says) the world's worst ladies' hairdresser.

Then at 19, be was trying to chat up this girl and she took him to see a play, a thing unheard-of in his family: his father kept a chip shop. He had a terrible night out but the girl persisted. So did her parents. "To walk into that house," he says, "and find that people who spoke posh weren't remote was a great encouragement." They changed his life by leading him to books and urging him to go to a local college and take A-levels. Soon, in the back room light of his Kirkby hair salon, amazed at his own delight, he was writing essays about "Henry V" and George Orwell. He read all the literary reviews hoping their classiness would rub off and he would become a writer and wear tweeds and smoke a pipe ... It did not happen.

Now, he knows why. He had come from a culture which unterstands story-telling and has little use for literary abstractions. He makes a firm distinction between words intended to be read and those meant to be heard. The songs he has composed and sung in the folk idiom, since he was 20 or so, established him in the clubs and on radio – these too were addressed to the listener's ear and not the readers eye. However, he married that girl, and today they have three children, though it took time for him

at heart *here:* in mind, *i.e.* he is thinking of the working class when he writes **apprehensive** nervous **hobnail boots** (hobnailed boots) heavy boots worn by workers on building sites etc. (the hobnail is a sort of heavy nail used to attach the soles to the boots) **to champion** to stick up for s.th., to defend s.th. **Jeremy Irons** famous English actor in films and plays *e.g. Brideshead Revisited, Waterlands* **untapped** not yet exploited *here:* the people for whom no plays have been written (plays had been traditionally written for the upper and middle classes) **it cost him dear** *G.* es kam ihn teuer zu stehen **to chat s.o. up** • to talk or to flirt with s.o. *G.* jmd. anmachen **to persist** to keep trying, to not give up **to speak posh** • to speak with an upper class accent **delight** great joy **tweeds** clothing (usually a jacket) made of tweed (a type of material made from wool)

to find that the theatre was a great arena for the telling of stories.

His self-discovery came when he was pressed to put together a play in a week for a student production, at St. Katherine's College, Liverpool. As a result the local Everyman Theatre started commissioning him, and not long after, in 1974, his Beatles play for them, "John, Paul, George, Ringo and Bert" transferred to London, ran a year of Shaftesbury Avenue and won awards as the best musical of the year.

For a current sample of Russell's work, Londoners can see "Stags and Hens", now at the Young Vic, a play he wrote in 1978 when a Fellow of Creative Writing at Manchester Polytechnic.

"Blood Brothers", a homespun and somewhat creaky yarn about twin siblings who grow up in different social milieux and end one killing the other, currently on tour in a new production, returns to the West End in September.
He says: "There is my audience, and there are those who live for Shakespeare and Beethoven's 9th. But it's not an either-or situation. It's a question of saying 'That is fine, that is catering for its audience'. But there's another audience out there, unwilling to make any concessions to the accepted way of watching theatre.
I don't want my plays to appeal only to those who go every night of the week, but also to people who have never been to a theatre – by engaging them at a level they trust, understand and value. The best way is to have a story to tell. I always come back to that. The lights go down, the curtain goes up, and you are with this story for two hours. That ritual, that magic, when it happens, welds the most wildly different people into one."

The Daily Telegraph, July 16, 1984

7. Twenty Years of Willy Russell

1972	When the Reds (stage)
	King of the Castle (television)
1974	John, Paul, George, Ringo and Bert (stage)
	Death of a Young Young Man (television)
1975	Breezeblock Park (stage)
1977	Our Day Out (television)
1978	One for the Road (stage)
1979	Daughters of Albion (television)
	Stags & Hens (stage)
1980	Educating Rita (stage)
	One Summer (television)
1983	Blood Brothers (stage)
	Educating Rita (film)
1988	Shirley Valentine (stage)
1989	Shirley Valentine (screenplay)
1990	Dancing thru' the Dark (screenplay)

to cater for to produce what is needed or desired by s.o. or s.th. *here:* to produce a play that is suitable for the intended audience **to engage s.o.** to occupy or attract the attention of s.o. **to weld** to unite

8. Interview with Willy Russell (Excerpt)

Liverpool, 9 March 1982

(ARG: Albert-Reiner Glaap; WR: Willy Russell)

ARG: Seeing the play one gets the impression Rita takes the Open University course in order to qualify for something else, to get what might be a ticket enabling her to enter higher social strata. Is that right?

WR: No, I don't think she wants to enter, for the sake of it, a higher social stratum. I think that what her instinct tells her is that if she enters this *other* stratum, not necessarily *higher*, but this other stratum, she can feed the element inside her which is not being fed in her present social stratum. She says how hungry she is for education. She does want to be able to sit down and discuss books and art and music and to be spiritually fed and, to stay in the metaphor, she feels that she's starving in her present social stratum, that it's arid and that if she moves in this other social stratum it will be some sort of oasis. This was certainly something I felt before I went back to education. I overvalued to a ludicrous extent the idea of education, what, you know, college and higher education was and went through a period being very much like Rita, you know, being very bored and suffering from "art in the head". I used to stop people on buses and ask them what they thought of Chekhov which was very boring for them. Poor souls on the buses.

ARG: The question that I asked myself when reading the play was: Can education be dealt with on its own? Shouldn't it be linked up with politics, somehow?

WR: I think the play is political and I think it's linked to politics.

ARG: Could you enlarge on that? What is the political aspect of it? I mean developments and changes in the field of educa-

strata ['strɑːtə; 'streɪtə] *G.* Schichten (*singular* = stratum) **for the sake of it** *G.* um der Sache willen **spiritual** ['spɪrɪtʃʊəl] *G.* geistig **arid** ['ærɪd] dry **ludicrous** ['luːdikrəs] completely ridiculous **souls** *G.* Seelen; Leute **to link up with** to join up to **to enlarge** to speak or write more fully about

tion are somehow predetermined, as it were, by political decisions, aren't they?

WR: Yes, they are. When I became a teacher (this is probably a sort of side issue but it might answer the question), when I became a teacher I went into teaching because I thought I could actually radically alter certain situations and could effect some sort of change. I thought that teaching was a potent political tool. I found out when I got into education that education was the tail of the dog which was being wagged by the political animal and that one was mostly ineffectual as a teacher because you were the branches, you weren't the roots of the trees and whatever was decided at root level you had to implement. There was certain leeway within that, you know, one could, if you like, counter-influence once one was in the classroom, but in the broadest sense of the word one was fairly impotent as a teacher given the prevailing political party of the day. What I mean when I say that the play is political is not political in an obviously ... I mean it doesn't discuss the politics of education; it's the politics of the people involved in the play, and it's political because it's discussing class in this country.

to predetermine to settle in advance **as it were** in a way **side issue** ['ɪʃuː] secondary matter **to effect** to bring about **potent** powerful **tool** instrument **to wag** *G.* wedeln **ineffectual** *G.* nicht wirkungsvoll **to implement** to carry out **certain leeway** a certain amount of freedom of action; *G.* Spielraum **prevailing** herrschend **the people involved** *G.* die Betreffenden

9. Interview with Willy Russell

Liverpool, 16 October 1996

(ARG: Albert-Reiner Glaap; WR: Willy Russell)

ARG: A playscript is a blueprint, a musical score in contrast to a novel that you write for readers who can immediately read it.

WR: Yes, that is true. A play on paper is merely an expression of intention. And until it goes through the process of realisation it does not truly exist. I enjoy reading plays, in fact I'm able to mount the production in my head when I read. But generally speaking, a play is not a play until it's up there on the stage and a novel is a novel when it's there on the page. But I'm trying to write novels where the reader feels "read to" rather than reading. There are great differences between writing a novel and writing a play. But it's not completely separate. I can see the connections with drama. If one thinks of *Shirley Valentine,* for example, Shirley stands there on a stage and tells you her story. Raymond, in one of my novels, happens to use the page to tell you a story, and Ralph uses the page to tell you his version of the story. So they're not that wildly different. I do, for example, on the tour that I'm doing with the poets, read two excerpts from the Raymond novel on the stage and it works perfectly well as a piece of staged work.

ARG: Thinking of your development as a writer you have written plays, you still write plays, you have written filmscripts and now you are writing a novel.

WR: Yes, I've never been afraid of that. We live in a period now where one is often criticised for employing a myriad of forms. The English phrase is, "He's spreading himself too thinly". But I've never been afraid of the notion of "renaissance man". I think it's very good that a man can write a ballad and fence, that a man can go out onto the battlefield, that he can soldier, that he can love, and that he can write sonnets. That completeness is something that I've never shied away from. Maybe the critics would say, "Yes despite that, you have spread yourself too thinly". But I'm sorry, that's the way I am, that's the way I'm going to write. I find it odd, in many respects, to be writing novels at this point in my life when in almost every periodical or arts programme I read or look at, I hear somebody talking

blueprint a detailed plan **musical score** *G.* Partitur **to mount s.th.** to organize s.th. **myriad** [ˈmɪrɪəd] a very large number **to shy away from doing s.th.** to avoid doing s.th. **periodical** magazine

about the death of the novel and how the screenplay is the art form of the latter end of the twentieth century. And here's me turning away from screenplays, the supposed cutting edge form, and going back to what people are trying to say is an outmoded, outdated form. Of course, it's not an outmoded, outdated form. That is just a sort of handy debate at the moment. Although I *do* love the way that screenplays have influenced the novel. I *do* like novels which are reduced to their essentials, cut down to the absolute leanest. I find it good to read a novel that is almost totally written in dialogue the way a screenplay would be.

ARG: The good thing about your plays, take *Educating Rita* for example, is that they're not really structured in the traditional way.

WR: No, they're not. I was always worried about the structure of *Educating Rita*. It has form, it has unity of time and space – but in a way that was not immediately obvious to me when I wrote it. And when I saw it I thought, oh yes, it goes over an arc of a year, or whatever, or an arc of three years, however you want to see it. It just had to be written in consecutive scenes, that play.

ARG: Thinking of the period between when *Educating Rita* was written and 1996 and looking at it from the point of view of those who read or see the play, have the reactions to the play had some kind of impact on you and what sort of feedback do you get from the audiences?

WR: Well, the enormous feedback I still get to this day is from people who feel moved to write to me, to tell me how this play has profoundly affected them and their lives, made them seek education and fulfilment through education. I really do meet lots and lots of people who say, "I'm Rita". I'm sure that those people would have changed anyway, but maybe the fact that Rita existed gave them a means of articulating more quickly or moving more quickly to change their own lives. And one of the interesting things is that now it's a phrase that's entered the English language. "Doing a Rita" entered the language a long, long time ago, just like "doing a Shirley Valentine". You often see headlines in papers: "Educating Rita Story", "Educating Rita Girl", or "Shirley Valentine Woman Goes to…"; you know the sort of stuff. I made a speech last year. John Moores University here had made me a Fellow and I had to speak to a graduate ceremony. And I was aware that John Moores University has a

cutting edge most modern, most recent **Fellow** member *here:* member of the John Moores University

higher intake of mature students than any other university in this country – over 50 percent of its students are mature students – and so as part of my speech I addressed myself to *Educating Rita*. I began by saying to this audience that one of the wonderful things about *Educating Rita* is that it is now, strictly speaking in England, a play that is out of date because when I wrote that play – and we're talking about 1979 when I first sat down to write it, more than fifteen years ago – the idea of a working class man or woman, aged twenty-six, returning to education really was quite unusual and radical. I knew from my own experience, having gone back to college aged twenty-one to do O-levels and A-levels, that it was seen as a very strange thing to do. A twenty-one-year-old in classes with sixteen-year-olds doing what he should have been doing when he was sixteen. I stood out like a real sore thumb, me and two others who were at that college. And the same was still true when I wrote *Educating Rita*. If you wanted to get back into education – if you felt that you'd not done or had what you wanted from school – it was exceptional. The reason I was saying to this gathering that I considered it now, thankfully, to be out of date, was that since *Educating Rita,* and partly because of *Educating Rita,* we now have in this country a whole panoply of "return to learn" schemes. The idea of education being something for life, and to be conducted throughout life, is now central in British educational culture. And I was able to mark the fact that here I was receiving an award from a university that has a higher intake of mature students so that in its specific terms the play is, strictly speaking, out of date. Of course, in its universal terms it's not because you can't date someone's struggle for realisation and self-fulfilment.

ARG: To hang on to what you've just told me: Would you, today, write a completely new play or would you say, well, this is the play but I could add something that really points out how things have developed?

WR: No, I wouldn't touch the play at all. The play was written in its time and it must stand.

ARG: And it's supposed to be a period play in that it deals with that particular era; and although things have changed it should be taken for what it has always been.

mature student older student, s.o. who did not go straight to university after school **O-levels** *G.* vergleichbar mit der Mittleren Reife **A-levels** *G.* vergleichbar mit dem Abitur **to stick out like a sore thumb** to stand out, to be very obvious **a whole panoply** ['pænəplı] *G.* eine ganze Palette

WR: Let's say if I were to be involved in a new mounting of the play in London, I would probably, I suspect, want it to be as immediate as it could be. So at that point I might be tempted to get my pen out and change the specific references, the specific late nineteen-seventies references to Farrah Fawcett-Majors and what have you and make it more immediate, which one could do without in any sense damaging the centre of the play. It's a day's job to do. But I'm not prepared to do that for the myriad productions that are happening as we speak, because I'd just put a noose around my neck. If I did this year's updating, by next year certain references would be out of date, and I'd be constantly doing it.

ARG: What would you tell students in German secondary schools about *Educating Rita* now in 1996, fifteen years or so after the play was written? Would you say it is a play that's completely out of date?

WR: Well, no, I don't think it's at all out of date because of what I said about its universality. It's a play that's been constantly produced since the day it was written – not because of its specific nature, its specific issues, and setting, locale, and topicality. It's a play that's been produced because of the universality within that and, though I didn't know this when I was writing it, it's an ageless story that crosses all sorts of boundaries of class, language, race and whatever. I take that to indicate that there is this sort of universal heart at the centre of it. Just as in the way I will read plays from five hundred years ago, fifty years ago and there will be certain references that won't be as potent for me now as they were for the contemporary audience. But nevertheless I can understand what a tram in the middle of London meant for that play at that particular time and translate it into my own particular terms. For example with something like *A Streetcar Named Desire* we know, don't we, that that whole streetcar thing doesn't exist down there in the South the way it did when Tennessee Williams wrote his play. But that in no way diminishes the play. It would be a terrible thing to do to try and update that streetcar and make it into whatever the equivalent is today. As we watch it we are moved down to our souls because we're engaging in what drama should be – the condition of humanity.

ARG: The universal always comes through the particular. And we replace particulars with other particulars but that doesn't mean anything as far as the universal message is concerned. How do you com-

noose *G.* Schlinge

pare the film and the stage version? The stage version really appeals to the audience's imagination, doesn't it, and the people sitting in the theatre have got to people the scene themselves which is a challenging, interesting and intriguing kind of job, whereas the film, with all the off-stage characters coming in, takes people more or less on what I would call a conducted tour and there's hardly anything left for them to do. Would you agree?

WR: Yes. That is the nature of film, that is the inescapable nature of film. It is a literal medium. One knew the term when one sat down to write the screenplay. I knew I was writing for a mainstream production, so I wasn't going to write it as an art film. And I wouldn't want to write it as an art film, anyway, because the majority of art films I see, I hate. Film is a big, popular, sprawling medium and I take that on board when I sit down to make a film. I'm not saying I don't really want to write that sort of film. I have to try and do what I can achieve within that big commercial world. So one accepted that one was working in a much more literal medium. But the stage version for me is always stronger, more potent, because it is not a literal medium, it is a poetic medium and one is able to achieve a level of poetry in the theatre with *Educating Rita* – no matter how good the film, and I watched it recently and wept I have to say, when I saw my children, my tiny children as they were then, I wept copiously, but that was obviously a kind of private reaction. I know people who just adore the film and are terribly moved by it, so I wouldn't in any sense denigrate the film. I think what the film does is by and large fine as a film, but it is not the play and it never could be the play.

ARG: I understand that in the very original version of *Educating Rita* there was no Frank.

WR: It was not a public or published version. It was never staged. It was a draft I sent to Peggy Ramsey, my agent. I'd written *Rita* and I didn't want anybody else's voice to get in the way of Rita. I couldn't allow anybody else's voice to get in the way. I had to write her story, her voice. So in that original draft Frank was an absolute vapid, colourless, almost off-stage cipher, a totally colourless man. Just occasionally he'd throw in a question or something in order to propel Rita's journey further along. He was an absolute foil. Having completed this first draft in which I'd completely realised Rita, I sent it to Peggy and thirty-six hours later I was at a meeting, I remember, in

copiously a lot **to denigrate** ['denɪgreɪt] to belittle, to say s.th. is worthless **cipher** figure of little or no importance *G. hier:* Statist

the Everyman Theatre and somebody came in to tell me there was a phonecall for me in the office and it was Peggy. She had read it and she thought Rita was wonderful and Frank totally useless. I was crushed, because it had taken me so long to write this play, not long in terms of time but it had taken so much out of me. The thought of having to go back to it depressed me beyond belief. It took me about eighteen or twenty hours before starting to think, "What I've got to do is I've got to write this play again, I've got to conceive Frank." Performance is often crucial in my work. I was having to give a reading later that week in a college here in Liverpool and I knew I wanted to read from *Educating Rita,* but knew I couldn't read from it with this vapid, colourless, non-realised Frank in it. I put the paper into the typewriter and instinctively I knew that if I was going to get Frank right, the play had to start with him. I was suddenly thrilled because I had a character here, not just a cipher. I had a man who does something on stage and immediately he has a background, immediately the audience will want to know. From then on, I think, I just typed for two days solid and Frank was alive in the play. And I sent it back to Peggy.

ARG: What does Liverpool mean to you, especially with reference to *Educating Rita?* I take it that this is not a play about specifically Liverpudlian issues, but Liverpool is a kind of metaphor.

WR: I find it difficult to talk on the subject of Liverpool. So many untruths have been said about Liverpool. I try and distance myself from that. Ridiculous claims have been made, there are so many prejudices in this country about Liverpool. On the one hand I feel terribly protective about my hometown and at other times I feel disgusted at the excesses of some its spokesmen. I adore Liverpool, but I also am very aware of its problems and its potential for chauvinism, wallowing nostalgia and loud-mouthedness for the sake of loud-mouthedness. One of the things I've done as a playwright very early on is I put the Liverpool idiom on stage in the theatre, not in poetry, not in song, not on television. But the language was not used in the theatre in order to seek universal truths. That's what I did, in retrospect. The language was not a language for "serious drama", but I did it. A couple of years after *Educating Rita* the Liverpool vernacular was being used widely on local radio-stations, commercial radio-stations, in advertisements and sitcoms and it no longer had for me

crucial very important **prejudice** *G.* Vorurteil **vernacular** spoken language or dialect **sitcom** (abbr.) situation comedy

the potency of this unused language. After *Blood Brothers* I started moving away from it a bit, because I felt the currency had become a bit debased. Rita does not specify Liverpool, you notice it just says northern. But patently the language of Rita is one of cast iron Liverpool.
ARG: When you say "language", what you mean is Scouse, or ...?
WR: Yes, it is Scouse. The language itself in the play is a journey. The journey of the play was partly a journey of language. I had to start with that sort of Liverpool thing.
It happens to be a fact that I live and work here, and I've always believed that if you write about any place well you are writing about everywhere. I've always revelled in the specifics of an area. But what you don't get in any of my plays, if you think about it, is particularly Liverpool references that would tie the play to Liverpool. You very rarely get buildings mentioned. In *Shirley Valentine* there is a reference to the Adelphi Hotel, but I write that knowing that if you've never been to Liverpool, you'd still understand. The Adelphi Hotel has a ring to it, it immediately gives you an image, it's a Greek word anyway.
ARG: There is one problem that foreign teachers and students may have: there are references to pieces of English literature that most of them, in our secondary schools, hardly ever read at home or in class.
WR: One of the crucial things about *Educating Rita* is that when I wrote it, I was immediately aware that writing a play set in a tutorial room of an academic institution with a professor of literature at the centre of it and a girl who wants to learn, could be written in such a way that it could fly completely over the heads of those people who did not live in that sort of world and knew nothing about that world. But I didn't want to write a play in which the Franks, as it were, in the audience enjoyed it, but the Ritas who stumbled into the theatre felt isolated. I wanted to write a play in such a way that my mother, an uneducated woman, could enjoy the play without feeling intimidated by the names. So the play is written in such a way that with no knowledge, or understanding of English literature, or references with which to connect things like *Howards End,* the poetry of William Blake, the Beat Poets or William Shakespeare, you could still understand what they represent, because you understand it through Rita's eyes. If you watch the scene where Rita compares and contrasts a Harold Robbins novel with the E.M. Forster, without

to revel ['revl] **in s.th/doing s.th.** to enjoy doing s.th., to take great delight in s.th.

having any knowledge of either of those books you'd sit there in the audience knowing that one was a piece of fiction that's considered to be cheap pulp fiction and the other was regarded as a highly esteemed piece of English Literature. I could have put invented authors with invented titles in that play, it wouldn't make a scrap of difference. To study *Educating Rita* you do not need to have a working knowledge of *Howards End.*

ARG: Does this also apply to the Open University as an educational institution? We, in Germany, have the *Fernuniversität,* but that is not quite an equivalent to the Open University.

WR: Again you could watch the play and not lose anything of it without having any understanding whatsoever of the Open University, because it's a human story. It's not the paraphernalia that surround it that's crucial. It's interesting and one should get inquisitive of all those details, just as I would, if I became immersed in an author's work, I'd want to know everything related to it. In terms of the theatre, which is not an academic exercise, the play works without any knowledge of those other authors.

ARG: One of the main differences between the screenplay and the stageplay, it occurred to me, is that in the film the relationship between Rita and Frank is more a relationship between Rita and Frank as human beings and not so much a relationship between tutor and student. How do you feel about that?

WR: That was not intentional, because I felt that the relationship between them as human beings was very strong in the play anyway and all the stronger for being restrained, consciously restrained. I think an inevitable by-product of the film, where you see those characters in all sorts of different locations, where you have to block them in all sorts of different bodily attitudes towards one and the other, and the fact of Michael Caine playing that particular role, all those things have a bearing on that. You're right actually, it probably does feel far more of a human relationship in the movie, but I didn't consciously sit down to write that in.

pulp fiction books or magazines of poor or cheap quality **paraphernalia** [ˌpærəfəˈneiliə] *G.* Zubehör, Utensilien **to immerse oneself in s.th.** to involve oneself deeply, to be absorbed by s.th.

10. A Touch of Working Class

The lead character grows up in a working-class family in the north of England. She takes a job as a ladies' hairdresser, hankers for more out of life, scrambles against the odds for an education and ends up drunk on knowledge. If this sounds like the plot of *Educating Rita,* a pleasing and successful new film, it is. But it's also the story – in rough outline – of the film's creator, Willy Russell, a plain-speaking Liverpool hairdresser turned playwright who himself might have walked straight out of the pages of George Bernard Shaw.

Russell, 36, has made an extraordinary success out of attacking the lingering biases in the British class system. And he does so with wit and style. In terms of audience totals, he is the third most popular playwright in Britain today (after Shakespeare and Alan Ayckbourn). The low-budget *Educating Rita* which originated as a West End play, has already earned 58.7 million in the United States alone. *Blood Brothers,* which the London arts magazine Time Out called "the best British musical since *Jesus Christ Superstar*" closed last month only because the theatre had another commitment. But it will reopen on tour next spring and may be made into a movie. Both *Educating Rita* and *Blood Brothers* deal with the theme of "two nations" – a Britain conspicuously divided into a deprived, socialist-minded north and a prosperous, conservative south. Liverpool is only three hours from London by train, but decades away in the quality of life. Even *Blood Brothers* dramatically prospers on fluid music and clever lyrics. The play tells of twins separated at birth, one to grow up in the slums, the other in the comfort of the managerial class. The twins are drawn to each other as boys, unaware of their genetic link. But as they grow older, the realities of class pry them apart.

Educating Rita, on the other hand, shows that the system can be breached. Rita, 26, played energetically by Julie Walters, enrolls in a university extension course, hoping it will open the door to a life beyond a dull job, evenings at the pub and a husband who only wants her to get pregnant. She is tutored, Pygmalion-style, by Frank (Michael Caine), a middle-aged don who relies on whisky for the kick he used to get from Coleridge. As Frank and Rita spar and joust their way through E.M. Forster and William Blake, class barriers begin to crumble, with each of them shedding a lot of preconceptions along the way.

The play's author discovered education himself when he was already in his 20s. The son of an eccentric, bookish

lead character the main character in a play or film **to hanker for** to want, to dream of **to scramble against the odds** to struggle to achieve s.th. although everyone thinks she/he is unlikely to succeed **lingering biases** prejudices that are taking a long time to disappear **audience totals** the amount of people going to the theatre overall **to be deprived** *here:* without much money. Historically the north of England has been considered poorer than the south **spar and joust** [dʒəʊst] two types of fighting: sparring is when two boxers practise with each other, jousting is when two people try to knock each other off a horse with a lance *here:* they are struggling to work through Blake and Forster **to shed a lot of preconceptions** to get rid of a lot of ideas that one has had **bookish** fond of reading

coal miner, he had left school at 15 with a dismal academic record and a vague, fanciful dream of becoming a writer. As a hairdresser, Russell scribbled poetry between coiffures. Like many of his Liverpool friends, he became entranced by the music of a group of lads known as "The Beatles," and began writing ballads and protest songs himself. The people he soon met in the music world convinced him that he could be a novelist – if he got an education.

After running into a series of closed doors, Russell was accepted in 1968 at a local college – where his writing immediately stagnated. "It was only when I gave up this 'art in the head' period of trying to be Graham Greene that I recognized that I had something valuable – my own working-class, story-telling culture," he says. From that point, Russell's road to success was remarkably short. His first three stage plays premiered at the Edinburgh Fringe Festival in 1972. Then his pithy, unromanticized version of the Beatles saga, "John, Paul, George, Ringo ... and Bert" won the London Evening Standard's award for "best musical of the year."

Russell's success hardly seems to have changed his style. He wears his hair long, speaks in a thick Liverpudlian accent and liberally spices his conversation with what Mickey, the working-class twin in *Blood Brothers,* calls "the F word." Liverpool with its gritty heritage, gives Russell's writing its edge, and he has no intention of leaving. "The south is soft," he says with contempt. "London is a terribly closed little society."

Pretensions: But Russell is not averse to knocking his own roots. *Breeze-block Park,* first staged in 1975, mounts a harsh attack on the pretensions and mindless diversions of the northern working class. Russell is a self-described socialist, but there are no stereotype working-class heroes or capitalist villains in his dramas. "Didactic plays I can admire as part of the politics industry," he says, "but they ain't good plays."

Liverpool's latest famous son isn't sure what he will do next. With *Blood Brothers,* suddenly a hot cinematic property, he wants to avoid a repeat of *Educating Rita,* where he and director Lewis Gilbert bought back the movie rights after Columbia Pictures wanted to tamper with the story. Nevertheless, once he sits down, at the typewriter again, the playwright says there's no telling what will emerge. "Rita just walked onto the paper, then she strolled around for 14 pages before I knew where she was going", he laughs. But chances are that both she – and her creator – will end up having gone farther than a young man named Willy Russell ever imagined.

Ronald Henkoff in Liverpool

dismal [ˈdɪzməl] very bad **fanciful** using imagination rather than reason or logic **coiffure** [kwɑːˈfjʊə(r)] hairstyle **road to success** the way towards achieving success **Edinburgh Fringe Festival** a yearly festival of alternative and experimental drama and comedy **pithy** concise and fully of meaning **gritty** coarse, raw **to give s.th. its edge** to give s.th. impact **soft** • weak, stupid **to be averse to** to be against, to be opposed to **knocking** • criticizing **to mount an attack on** to be very critical of **villain** criminal *G.* Bösewicht

11. Substance, Wit and Style Characterize Performance

"If you're looking for a show with substance, wit and style this summer ... I urge you – no implore you ... get on down to Georgetown to see "Educating Rita". Superbly produced by the Kings Playhouses' Roy S. Cameron and Derek Martin – "Educating Rita" is a play that entertains, enlightens and even educates. I know, I know ... you're on your vacation and it's summertime and you don't want to be educated ... Don't worry – school was never like this. This is theatre with a capital T. Frank is a tutor of English in his fifties whose disillusioned outlook on life drives him to drink as he buries himself in his books. Enter Rita. She is a forthright 26 year old who is hungry for education. Rita quickly wins over the very reticent teacher by her native shrewdness and her refusal to accept secondhand academic opinions. In the course of the play she gives Frank a new lease on life by making him believe in himself once again.

That in a nutshell is the story. But wait, there is so much more. Very rarely have I seen a play that is so rich in craftsmanship and effortless brilliance. The dialogue is intelligent and stimulating. The characters are multi-dimensional and clear as a bell. By the end of the play you feel as though you've known Frank and Rita all of your life. Eric Rieber and Janice Nutter are wonderful together as the mismatched romantic adversaries. Miss Nutter has the better of the two roles and she absolutely shines. If you have seen the movie I think you'll agree that she is even better than Julie Walters who received accolades for her performance. She is also stunningly beautiful ... you can really understand why Frank falls for her. I definitely did ... and I think you will too. Mr. Rieber is an endearingly rumpled professor and he delivers his cogent and witty lines with believable British tones and makes Frank the failed poet a truly memorable character. Roy S. Cameron's direction was professional and sensitive. His staging of this two character comedy ably demonstrates that he is a gifted pro and is a natural in the theatre. The costumes were excellent ... especially Miss Nutter's. She looked fabulous. Congratulations to Melinda

wit humour **to implore** to beg, to ask strongly **forthright** straightforward, clear and honest in speech and manner **reticent** ['retisnt] not revealing one's thoughts or feelings easily **shrewdness** from shrewd: having good judgement and common sense **to give s.o. a new lease on life •** to give s.o. new enthusiasm for things **adversaries** ['ædvəsərɪ] opponents in a contest **accolade** praise, approval **endearingly rumpled** *G.* liebevoll zerzaust **cogent** ['kəʊdʒənt] convincing, strong **to be a natural** to have a natural talent or ability for s.th.

Walker for her choice of clothes. But my highest compliments are for Gene Gibbons and Heather Sherman. The set and light design were magnificent. His set is the best I've seen this or any other summer ... including the Confederation Centre. It is such a pleasure to see this kind of superb theatre complimented by such intelligent and artful settings. It's a wonder how they did this on such a small budget. "Educating Rita" is a play for couples or singles young and old, the cynical or the innocent. If you must see only one play this summer see this one ... it's marvelous theatre."

Don Wright, Theatre Reviewer
CBC Charlottetown July, 1988

to be complimented by to be made complete by. Things which complement each other are said to go together well, *e.g.* coffee and cream **Charlottetown** the capital of the province Prince Edward Island/Canada

FICTIONAL TEXTS

1. Bernard Shaw*, Pygmalion

Act Two

[...]

Mrs Pearce *(hesitating, evidently perplexed)* A young woman asks to see you, sir.

Higgins A young woman! What does she want?

Mrs Pearce Well, sir, she says youll be glad to see her when you know what she's come about. She's quite a common girl, sir. Very common indeed. I should have sent her away, only I thought perhaps you wanted her to talk into your machines. I hope Ive not done wrong; but really you see such queer people sometimes – youll excuse me. I'm sure, sir –

Higgins Oh, thats all right, Mrs Pearce. Has she an interesting accent?

Mrs Pearce Oh, something dreadful, sir, really. I dont know how you can take an interest in it.

Higgins *(to Pickering)* Lets have her up. Shew her up, Mrs Pearce *(he rushes across to his working table and picks out a cylinder to use on the phonograph).*

Mrs Pearce *(only half resigned to it)* Very well, sir. It's for you to say. *(She goes downstairs).*

Higgins This is rather a bit of luck. I'll shew you how I make records. We'll set her talking; and I'll take it down first in Bell's Visible Speech; then in broad Romic; and then we'll get her on the phonograph so that you can turn her on as often as you like with the written transcript before you.

Mrs Pearce *(returning)* This is the young woman, sir.

The flower girl enters in state. She has a hat with three ostrich feathers, orange, sky-blue, and red. She has a nearly clean apron and the shoddy coat has been tidied a little. The pathos of this deplorable figure, with its innocent vanity and consequential air, touches Pickering, who has already straightened himself in the presence of Mrs Pearce. But as to Higgins, the only distinction he makes between men and women is that when he is neither bullying nor exclaiming to the

queer strange **Romic** a sytem for a phonetic alphabet **transcript** written copy, written record **ostrich** [ˈɒstrɪtʃ] Strauß **shoddy** of no good quality **deplorable** awful

* The Society of Authors on behalf of the Bernard Shaw Estate require that the author's name should appear as Bernard Shaw, not George Bernard Shaw

heavens against some feather-weight cross, he coaxes women as a child coaxes its nurse when it wants to get anything out of her.

Higgins *(brusquely, recognizing her with unconcealed disappointment, and at once, babylike, making an intolerable grievance of it)* Why, this is the girl I jotted down last night. She's no use: Ive got all the records I want of the Lisson Grove lingo; and I'm not going to waste another cylinder on it. *(To the girl)* Be off with you: I dont want you.

The Flower Girl Dont you be so saucy. You aint heard what I come for yet. *(To Mrs Pearce, who is waiting at the door for further instructions)* Did you tell him I come in a taxi?

Mrs Pearce Nonsense, girl! what do you think a gentleman like Mr Higgins cares what you came in?

The Flower Girl Oh, we are proud! He aint above giving lessons, not him: I heard him say so. Well, I aint come here to ask for any compliment; and if my money's not good enough I can go elsewhere.

Higgins Good enough for what?

The Flower Girl Good enough for yə-oo. Now you know, dont you? I'm coming to have lessons, I am. And to pay for em tə-oo: make no mistake.

Higgins *(stupent)* Well!!! *(Recovering his breath with a gasp)* What do you expect me to say to you?

The Flower Girl Well, if you was a gentleman, you might ask me to sit down, I think. Dont I tell you I'm bringing you business?

Higgins Pickering: shall we ask this baggage to sit down, or shall we throw her out of the window?

The Flower Girl *(running away in terror to the piano, where she turns at bay)* Ah-ah-oh-ow-ow-ow-oo! *(Wounded and whimpering)* I wont be called a baggage when Ive offered to pay like any lady.

Motionless, the two men stare at her from the other side of the room, amazed.

Pickering *(gently)* But what is it you want?

The Flower Girl I want to be a lady in a flower shop stead of sellin at the corner of Tottenham Court Road. But they wont take me unless I can talk more genteel. He said he could teach me. Well,

to coax s.o. to gently persuade s.o. **brusque** [bruːsk] rough **grievance** complaint, protest **lingo** jargon; way of speaking **saucy** rude **stupent** (alte Form von **stupefied**) amazed **genteel** [dʒenˈtiːl] politely, *here:* in the style of the upper social classes

here I am ready to pay him – not asking any favor – and he treats me zif I was dirt.

Mrs Pearce How can you be such a foolish ignorant girl as to think you could afford to pay Mr Higgins?

The Flower Girl Why shouldnt I? I know what lessons cost as well as you do; and I'm ready to pay.

Higgins How much?

The Flower Girl *(coming back to him, triumphant)* Now youre talking! I thought youd come off it when you saw a chance of getting back a bit of what you chucked at me last night. *(Confidentially)* Youd had a drop in, hadnt you?

Higgins *(peremptorily)* Sit down.

The Flower Girl Oh, if youre going to make a compliment of it –

Higgins *(thundering at her)* Sit down.

Mrs Pearce *(severely)* Sit down, girl. Do as youre told.

The Flower Girl Ah-ah-ah-ow-ow-oo! *(She stands, half rebellious, half-bewildered).*

Pickering *(very courteous)* Wont you sit down? *(He places the stray chair near the hearthrug between himself and Higgins).*

The Flower Girl *(coyly)* Dont mind if I do. *(She sits down. Pickering returns to the hearthrug).*

Higgins Whats your name?

The Flower Girl Liza Doolittle.

Higgins *(declaiming gravely)*
Eliza, Elizabeth, Betsy and Bess,
They went to the woods to get a bird's nes':

Pickering They found a nest with four eggs in it:

Higgins They took one apiece, and left three in it.

They laugh heartily at their own fun.

Liza Oh, dont be silly.

Mrs Pearce *(placing herself behind Eliza's chair)*
You mustnt speak to the gentleman like that.

Liza Well, why wont he speak sensible to me?

Higgins Come back to business. How much do you propose to pay me for the lessons?

Liza Oh, I know whats right. A lady friend of mine gets French lessons for eighteenpence an hour from a real French gentleman. Well, you wouldnt have the face to ask me the same for teaching

zif • as if **to have a drop in** • to be slightly drunk **hearthrug** ['hɑːθrʌg] small carpet in front of a fireplace **coyly** pretending to be shy **to have the face** to be impudent enough

me my own language as you would for French; so I wont give more than a shilling. Take it or leave it.

Higgins *(walking up and down the room, rattling his keys and his cash in his pockets)* You know, Pickering, if you consider a shilling, not as a simple shilling, but as a percentage of this girl's income, it works out as fully equivalent to sixty or seventy guineas from a millionaire.

Pickering How so?

Higgins Figure it out. A millionaire has about £150 a day. She earns about half-a-crown.

Liza *(haughtily)* Who told you I only –

Higgins *(continuing)* She offers me two-fifths of her day's income for a lesson. Two-fifths of a millionaire's income for a day would be somewhere about £60. It's handsome. By George, it's enormous! it's the biggest offer I ever had.

Liza *(rising, terrified)* Sixty pounds! What are you talking about? I never offered you sixty pounds. Where would I get –

Higgins Hold your tongue.

Liza *(weeping)* But I aint got sixty pounds. Oh –

Mrs Pearce Dont cry, you silly girl. Sit down. Nobody is going to touch your money.

Higgins Somebody is going to touch you, with a broomstick, if you dont stop snivelling. Sit down.

[...]

Act Three

[...]

Higgins *(rising hastily and running to Mrs Higgins)* Here she is, mother. *(He stands on tiptoe and makes signs over his mother's head to Eliza to indicate to her which lady is her hostess).*

Eliza, who is exquisitely dressed, produces an impression of such remarkable distinction and beauty as she enters that they all rise, quite fluttered. Guided by Higgins's signals, she comes to Mrs Higgins with studied grace.

Liza *(speaking with pedantic correctness of pronunciation and great beauty of tone)* How do you do, Mrs Higgins? *(She gasps slightly in making sure of the H in Higgins, but is quite successful).* Mr Higgins told me I might come.

haughtily proudly **to snivel** to cry (especially young children)

Mrs Higgins *(cordially)* Quite right: I'm very glad indeed to see you.
Pickering How do you do, Miss Doolittle?
Liza *(shaking hands with him)* Colonel Pickering, is it not?
Mrs Eynsford Hill I feel sure we have met before, Miss Doolittle. I remember your eyes.
Liza How do you do? *(She sits down on the ottoman gracefully in the place just left vacant by Higgins).*
Mrs Eynsford Hill *(introducing)* My daughter Clara.
Liza How do you do?
Clara *(impulsively)* How do you do? *(She sits down on the ottoman beside Eliza, devouring her with her eyes).*
Freddy *(coming to their side of the ottoman)* Ive certainly had the pleasure.
Mrs Eynsford Hill *(introducing)* My son Freddy.
Liza How do you do?
Freddy bows and sits down in the Elizabethan chair, infatuated.
Higgins *(suddenly)* By George, yes: it all comes back to me! *(They stare at him).* Covent Garden! *(Lamentably)* What a damned thing!
Mrs Higgins Henry, please! *(He is about to sit on the edge of the table)* Dont sit on my writing-table: youll break it.
Higgins *(sulkily)* Sorry.
He goes to the divan, stumbling into the fender and over the fire-irons on his way; extricating himself with muttered imprecations; and finishing his disastrous journey by throwing himself so impatiently on the divan that he almost breaks it. Mrs Higgins looks at him, but controls herself and says nothing.
A long and painful pause ensues.
Mrs Higgins *(at last, conversationally)* Will it rain, do you think?
Liza The shallow depression in the west of these islands is likely to move slowly in an easterly direction. There are no indications of any great change in the barometrical situation.
Freddy Ha! ha! how awfully funny!
Liza What is wrong with that, young man? I bet I got it right.
Freddy Killing!

cordially in a friendly way **ottoman** long, slightly circular type of sofa with no back or arms **to devour s.th.** to eat s.th. greedily **to be infatuated** to be full of an intense feeling of adoration **lamentably** sorrowfully, regretfully **sulky** *G.* schmollend, eingeschnappt **divan** [dɪˈvæn] couch **fender** *G.* Kamingitter **to extricate** to pull out **imprecation** oath, curse **to ensue** to follow

Mrs Eynsford Hill I'm sure I hope it wont turn cold. Theres so much influenza about. It runs right through our whole family regularly every spring.

Liza *(darkly)* My aunt died of influenza: so they said.

Mrs Eynsford Hill *(clicks her tongue sympathetically)*!!!

Liza *(in the same tragic tone)* But it's my belief they done the old woman in.

Mrs Higgins *(puzzled)* Done her in?

Liza Ye-e-e-e-es. Lord love you! Why should she die of influenza? She come through diphtheria right enough the year before. I saw her with my own eyes. Fairly blue with it, she was. They all thought she was dead; but my father he kept ladling gin down her throat til she came to so sudden that she bit the bowl off the spoon.

Mrs Eynsford Hill *(startled)* Dear me!

Liza *(piling up the indictment)* What call would a woman with that strength in her have to die of influenza? What become of her new straw hat that should have come to me? Somebody pinched it; and what I say is, them as pinched it done her in.

Mrs Eynsford Hill What does doing her in mean?

Higgins *(hastily)* Oh, thats the new small talk. To do a person in means to kill them.

Mrs Eynsford Hill *(to Eliza, horrified)* You surely dont believe that your aunt was killed?

Liza Do I not! Them she lived with would have killed her for a hat-pin, let alone a hat.

Mrs Eynsford Hill But it cant have been right for your father to pour spirits down her throat like that. It might have killed her.

Liza Not her. Gin was mother's milk to her. Besides, he'd poured so much down his own throat that he knew the good of it.

Mrs Eynsford Hill Do you mean that he drank?

Liza Drank! My word! Something chronic.

Mrs Eynsford Hill How dreadful for you!

Liza Not a bit. It never did him no harm what I could see. But then he did not keep it up regular. *(Cheerfully)* On the burst, as you might say, from time to time. And always more agreeable when he had a drop in. When he was out of work, my mother used to give

to do s.o. in • to kill s.o. **to ladle** *here:* to pour; **ladle** very large serving spoon for soup etc. **to come to** to wake up, become conscious **to pinch s.th.** • to steal s.th. **something chronic** • frequently, very often

him fourpence and tell him to go out and not come back until he'd drunk himself cheerful and loving-like. Theres lots of women has to make their husbands drunk to make them fit to live with. *(Now quite at her ease)* You see, it's like this. If a man has a bit of a conscience, it always takes him when he's sober; and then it makes him low-spirited. A drop of booze just takes that off and makes him happy. *(To Freddy, who is in convulsions of suppressed laughter)* Here! what are you sniggering at?

Freddy The new small talk. You do it so awfully well.

Liza If I was doing it proper, what was you laughing at? *(To Higgins)* Have I said anything I oughtnt?

Mrs Higgins *(interposing)* Not at all, Miss Doolittle.

Liza Well, thats a mercy, anyhow. *(Expansively)* What I always say is –

Higgins *(rising and looking at his watch)* Ahem!

Liza *(looking round at him; taking the hint; and rising)* Well: I must go. *(They all rise. Freddy goes to the door).* So pleased to have met you. Goodbye. *(She shakes hands with Mrs Higgins).*

Mrs Higgins Goodbye.

Liza Goodbye, Colonel Pickering.

Pickering Goodbye, Miss Doolittle. *(They shake hands).*

Liza *(nodding to the others)* Goodbye, all.

Freddy *(opening the door for her)* Are you walking across the Park, Miss Doolittle? If so –

Liza *(with perfectly elegant diction)* Walk! Not bloody likely. *(Sensation).* I am going in a taxi. *(She goes out).*

[...]

Act Four

[...]

Eliza tries to control herself and feel indifferent as she rises and walks across to the hearth to switch off the lights. By the time she gets there she is on the point of screaming. She sits down in Higgins's chair and holds on hard to the arms. Finally she gives way and flings herself furiously on the floor, raging.

Higgins *(in despairing wrath outside)* What the devil have I done with my slippers? *(He appears at the door).*

booze • alcohol **convulsions of laughter** *G.* Lachkrampf **wrath** [rɒθ] great anger

Liza *(snatching up the slippers, and hurling them at him one after the other with all her force)* There are your slippers. And there. Take your slippers; and may you never have a day's luck with them!

Higgins *(astounded)* What on earth –! *(He comes to her).* Whats the matter? Get up. *(He pulls her up).* Anything wrong?

Liza *(breathless)* Nothing wrong – with you. Ive won your bet for you, havnt I? Thats enough for you. *I* dont matter, I suppose.

Higgins You won my bet! You! Presumptuous insect! *I* won it. What did you throw those slippers at me for?

Liza Because I wanted to smash your face. I'd like to kill you, you selfish brute. Why didnt you leave me where you picked me out of – in the gutter? You thank God it's all over, and that now you can throw me back again there, do you? *(She crisps her fingers frantically).*

Higgins *(looking at her in cool wonder)* The creature is nervous, after all.

Liza *(gives a suffocated scream of fury, and instinctively darts her nails at his face)*!!

Higgins *(catching her wrists)* Ah! would you? Claws in, you cat. How dare you shew your temper to me? Sit down and be quiet. *(He throws her roughly into the easy-chair).*

Liza *(crushed by superior strength and weight)* Whats to become of me? Whats to become of me?

Higgins How the devil do I know whats to become of you? What does it matter what becomes of you?

Liza You dont care. I know you dont care. You wouldnt care if I was dead. I'm nothing to you – not so much as them slippers.

Higgins *(thundering)* Those slippers.

Liza *(with bitter submission)* Those slippers. I didnt think it made any difference now.

A pause. Eliza hopeless and crushed. Higgins a little uneasy.

Higgins *(in his loftiest manner)* Why have you begun going on like this? May I ask whether you complain of your treatment here?

Liza No.

Higgins Has anybody behaved badly to you? Colonel Pickering? Mrs Pearce? Any of the servants?

Liza No.

Higgins I presume you dont pretend that *I* have treated you badly?

to hurl s.th. to throw s.th. forcefully **presumptuous** too self-confident **suffocated scream** *G.* erstickter Schrei **lofty** seeming to be superior or proud

Liza No.

Higgins I am glad to hear it. *(He moderates his tone).* Perhaps youre tired after the strain of the day. Will you have a glass of champagne? *(He moves towards the door).*

Liza No. *(Recollecting her manners)* Thank you.

Higgins *(good-humored again)* This has been coming on you for some days. I suppose it was natural for you to be anxious about the garden party. But thats all over now. *(He pats her kindly on the shoulder. She writhes).* Theres nothing more to worry about.

Liza No. Nothing more for you to worry about. *(She suddenly rises and gets away from him by going to the piano bench, where she sits and hides her face).* Oh God! I wish I was dead.

Higgins *(staring after her in sincere surprise)* Why? In heaven's name, why? *(Reasonably, going to her)* Listen to me, Eliza. All this irritation is purely subjective.

Liza I dont understand. I'm too ignorant.

Higgins It's only imagination. Low spirits and nothing else. Nobody's hurting you. Nothing's wrong. You go to bed like a good girl and sleep it off. Have a little cry and say your prayers: that will make you comfortable.

Liza I heard your prayers. 'Thank God it's all over!'

Higgins *(impatiently)* Well, dont you thank God it's all over? Now you are free and can do what you like.

Liza *(pulling herself together in desperation)* What am I fit for? What have you left me fit for? Where am I to go? What am I to do? Whats to become of me?

Higgins *(enlightened, but not at all impressed)* Oh, thats whats worrying you, is it? *(He thrusts his hands into his pockets, and walks about in his usual manner, rattling the contents of his pockets, as if condescending to a trivial subject out of pure kindness).* I shouldnt bother about it if I were you. I should imagine you wont have much difficulty in settling yourself somewhere or other, though I hadnt quite realized that you were going away. *(She looks quickly at him: he does not look at her, but examines the dessert stand on the piano and decides that he will eat an apple).* You might marry, you know. *(He bites a large piece out of the apple and munches it noisily).* You see, Eliza, all men are not confirmed old bachelors like me and the Colonel. Most men are

to writhe [raɪð] to twist or roll about as if in discomfort **to thrust** to push violently
condescending *G.* herablassend

the marrying sort (poor devils!); and youre not bad-looking: it's quite a pleasure to look at you sometimes – not now, of course, because youre crying and looking as ugly as the very devil; but when youre all right and quite yourself, youre what I should call attractive. That is, to the people in the marrying line, you understand. You go to bed and have a good nice rest; and then get up and look at yourself in the glass; and you wont feel so cheap.

Eliza again looks at him, speechless, and does not stir.

The look is quite lost on him: he eats his apple with a dreamy expression of happiness, as it is quite a good one.

Higgins *(a genial afterthought occurring to him)* I daresay my mother could find some chap or other who would do very well.

Liza We were above that at the corner of Tottenham Court Road.

Higgins *(waking up)* What do you mean?

Liza I sold flowers. I didnt sell myself. Now youve made a lady of me I'm not fit to sell anything else. I wish youd left me where you found me.

Higgins *(slinging the core of the apple decisively into the grate)* Tosh, Eliza. Dont you insult human relations by dragging all this cant about buying and selling into it. You neednt marry the fellow if you dont like him.

Liza What else am I to do?

Higgins Oh, lots of things. What about your old idea of a florist's shop? Pickering could set you up in one: he has lots of money. *(Chuckling)* He'll have to pay for all those togs you have been wearing today; and that, with the hire of the jewellery, will make a big hole in two hundred pounds. Why, six months ago you would have thought it the millennium to have a flower shop of your own. Come! youll be all right. I must clear off to bed: I'm devilish sleepy. By the way, I came down for something: I forget what it was.

Liza Your slippers.

[...]

genial kind, pleasant **grate** fireplace **tosh** • rubbish **cant** insincere talk **togs** • clothes **millennium** *G.* höchstes Glücksgefühl

[...]

Higgins *(jumping up and walking about intolerantly)* Eliza: youre an idiot. I waste the treasures of my Miltonic mind by spreading them before you. Once for all, understand that I go my way and do my work without caring twopence what happens to either of us. I am not intimidated, like your father and your stepmother. So you can come back or go to the devil: which you please.

Liza What am I to come back for?

Higgins *(bouncing up on his knees on the ottoman and leaning over it to her)* For the fun of it. Thats why I took you on.

Liza *(with averted face)* And you may throw me out tomorrow if I dont do everything you want me to?

Higgins Yes, and you may walk out tomorrow if I dont do everything you want me to.

Liza And live with my stepmother?

Higgins Yes, or sell flowers.

Liza Oh! If I only could go back to my flower basket! I should be independent of both you and father and all the world! Why did you take my independence from me? Why did I give it up? I'm a slave now, for all my fine clothes.

Higgins Not a bit. I'll adopt you as my daughter and settle money on you if you like. Or would you rather marry Pickering?

Liza *(looking fiercely round at him)* I wouldnt marry you if you asked me; and youre nearer my age than what he is.

Higgins *(gently)* Than he is: not "than what he is".

Liza *(losing her temper and rising)* I'll talk as I like. Youre not my teacher now.

Higgins *(reflectively)* I dont suppose Pickering would, though. He's as confirmed an old bachelor as I am.

Liza Thats not what I want; and dont you think it. Ive always had chaps enough wanting me that way. Freddy Hill writes to me twice and three times a day, sheets and sheets.

Higgins *(disagreeably surprised)* Damn his impudence! *(He recoils and finds himself sitting on his heels).*

Liza He has a right to if he likes, poor lad. And he does love me.

Higgins *(getting off the ottoman)* You have no right to encourage him.

Miltonic mind a mind like John Milton (1608-1674), English poet, one of his most famous work is *Paradise Lost* **to avert** to turn away **impudence** rudeness

Liza Every girl has a right to be loved.

Higgins What! By fools like that?

Liza Freddy's not a fool. And if he's weak and poor and wants me, may be he'd make me happier than my betters that bully me and dont want me.

Higgins Can he make anything of you? Thats the point.

Liza Perhaps I could make something of him. But I never thought of us making anything of one another; and you never think of anything else. I only want to be natural.

Higgins In short, you want me to be as infatuated about you as Freddy? Is that it?

Liza No I dont. Thats not the sort of feeling I want from you. And dont you be too sure of yourself or of me. I could have been a bad girl if I'd liked. Ive seen more of some things than you, for all your learning. Girls like me can drag gentlemen down to make love to them easy enough. And they wish each other dead the next minute.

Higgins Of course they do. Then what in thunder are we quarrelling about?

Liza *(much troubled)* I want a little kindness. I know I'm a common ignorant girl, and you a book-learned gentleman; but I'm not dirt under your feet. What I done *(correcting herself)* what I did was not for the dresses and the taxis: I did it because we were pleasant together and I come – came – to care for you; not to want you to make love to me, and not forgetting the difference between us, but more friendly like.

Higgins Well, of course. Thats just how I feel. And how Pickering feels. Eliza: youre a fool.

Liza Thats not a proper answer to give me *(she sinks on the chair at the writing-table in tears).*

Higgins It's all youll get until you stop being a common idiot. If youre going to be a lady, youll have to give up feeling neglected if the men you know dont spend half their time snivelling over you and the other half giving you black eyes. If you cant stand the coldness of my sort of life, and the strain of it, go back to the gutter. Work til youre more a brute than a human being; and then cuddle and squabble and drink til you fall asleep. Oh, it's a fine life, the life of the gutter. It's real: it's warm: it's violent: you can feel it through the thickest skin: you can taste it and smell it without any training or any work. Not like Science and Literature and Classical Music and Philosophy and Art. You find me cold, unfeeling, selfish, dont you? Very well: be off with you to the sort of people you like. Marry some sentimental hog or other with lots of money, and a thick pair of lips to kiss you with and a thick pair of boots to kick you with. If you cant appreciate what youve got, youd better get what you can appreciate.

[...]

2. Arnold Wesker, Roots (1959)

Beatie. [...] I sit with Ronnie and his friends sometimes and I listen to them talk about things and you know I've never heard half of the words before.

Jenny. Don't he tell you what they mean?

Beatie. I get annoyed when he keep tellin' me – and he want me to ask.

(Imitates him half-heartedly now) 'Always ask, people love to tell you what they know, always ask and people will respect you.'

Jenny. And do you?

Beatie. No! I don't! An' you know why? Because I'm stubborn, I'm like Mother. I'm stubborn. Somehow I just can't bring myself to ask, and you know what? I go mad when I listen to them. As soon as they start to talk about things I don't know about or I can't understand I get mad. They sit there, casually talking, and suddenly they turn on you, abrupt. 'Don't you think?' they say. Like at school, pick on you and ask a question you ent ready for. Sometimes I don't say anything, sometimes I go to bed or leave the room. Like Jimmy – just like Jimmy.

Jenny. And what do Ronnie say to that then?

Beatie. He get mad too. 'Why don't you ask me woman, for God's sake why don't you ask me? Aren't I dying to tell you about things? Only ask!'

Jenny. And he's goin' to marry you?

Beatie. Why not?

Jenny. Well I'm sorry gal, you mustn't mind me saying this, but it don't seem to me like you two got much in common.

Beatie *(loudly)*. It's not true! We're in love!

Jenny. Well, you know.

Beatie *(softly)*. No, I don't know. I won't know till he come here. From the first day I went to work as waitress in the Dell Hotel and saw him working in the kitchen I fell in love – and I thought it was easy. I thought everything was easy. I chased him for three months with compliments and presents until I finally give myself to him. He never said he love me nor I didn't care but once he had taken me he seemed to think he was responsible for me and I told him no different. I'd *make* him love me I thought. I didn't know much about him except he was different and used to write most of the time. And then he went back to London and I followed him there. I've never moved far from home but I did for him and he felt all the time he couldn't leave me and I didn't tell him no different. And then I got to know more about him. He was interested in all the things I never even thought about. About politics and art and all that, and he tried to teach me. He's a socialist and he used to say you couldn't bring socialism to a country by making speeches, but perhaps you could pass it on to someone who was near you. So I pretended I was interested – but I didn't understand much. All the time he's trying to teach me but I can't take it Jenny. And yet, at the same time, I want to show I'm willing. I'm not used to learning. Learning was at school and that's finished with. [...]

In: The Wesker Trilogy (1960).
(Harmondsworth: Penguin 1977, pp. 94–95)

3. Charles Dickens, Hard Times (1854)

THE ONE THING NEEDFUL

"Now, what I want is Facts. Teach these boys and girls nothing but Facts. Facts alone are wanted in life. Plant nothing else, and root out everything else. You can only form the minds of reasoning animals upon Facts: nothing else will ever be of any service to them. This is the principle on which I bring up my own children, and this is the principle on which I bring up these children. Stick to Facts, Sir!"
"In this life, we want nothing but Facts, Sir; nothing but Facts!" The speaker, and the schoolmaster, and the third grown person, all backed a little, and swept with their eyes the inclined plane of little vessels then and there arranged in order, ready to have imperial gallons of facts poured into them until they were full to the brim.

(Harmondsworth: Penguin 1969, Chapter I, p. 47)

4. Thomas Hughes, Tom Brown's School Days (1857)

In no place in the world has individual character more weight than at a public school. Remember this, I beseech you, all you boys who are getting into the upper forms. Now is the time in all your lives probably when you may have more wide influence for good or evil on the society you live in than you ever can have again. Quit yourselves like men, then; speak up, and strike out if necessary for whatsoever is true, and manly, and lovely, and of good report; never try to be popular, but only to do your duty and help others to do theirs, and you may leave the tone of feeling in the school higher than you found it, and so be doing good, which no living soul can measure, to generations of your countrymen yet unborn. For boys follow one another in herds like sheep, for good or evil; they hate thinking, and have rarely any settled principles. Every school, indeed, has its own traditionary standard of right and wrong, which cannot be transgressed with impunity, marking certain things as low and blackguard, and certain others as lawful and right. This standard is ever varying, though it changes only slowly, and little by little; and, subject only to such standard, it is the leading boys for the time being who give the tone to all the rest, and make the School either a noble institution for the training of Christian Englishmen, or a place where a young boy will get more evil than he would if he were turned out to make his way in London streets, or anything between these two extremes.

(New York: Airmont Publishing Company 1968, pp. 135-136)

Note: This book was the beginning of a fashion in reading. Books about boys' and girls' public schools were so popular that some even appeared in comics. The ideas about public school life which they presented influenced generations of school children like Rita.

"Let Nature be your teacher:
Sweet is the lore which Nature brings;
Our meddling intellect
Mis-shapes the beauteous forms of things.
We murder to dissect –
Enough of Science and of Art;
Close up those barren leaves;
Come forth, and bring with you a heart
That watches and receives." – WORDSWORTH

(p. 192)

5. Muriel Spark, The Prime of Miss Jean Brodie (1961)

[...] 'I follow my principles of education and give of my best in my prime. The word "education" comes from the root *e* from *ex*, out, and *duco*, I lead. It means a leading out. To me education is a leading out of what is already there in the pupil's soul. To Miss Mackay it is a putting in of something that is not there, and that is not what I call education, I call it intrusion, from the Latin root prefix *in* meaning in and the stem *trudo*, I thrust. Miss Mackay's method is to thrust a lot of information into the pupil's head; mine is a leading out of knowledge, and that is true education as is proved by the root meaning. Now Miss Mackay has accused me of putting ideas into my girls' heads, but in fact that is *her* practice and mine is quite the opposite. Never let it be said that I put ideas into your heads. What is the meaning of education, Sandy?' [...](pp. 36 and 37)
Miss Brodie said, 'So I intend simply to point out to Miss Mackay that there is a radical difference in our principles of education. Radical is a word pertaining to roots – Latin *radix*, a root. We differ at root, the headmistress and I, upon the question whether we are employed to educate the minds of girls or to intrude upon them. We have had this argument before, but Miss Mackay is not, I may say, an outstanding logician. A logician is one skilled in logic. Logic is the art of reasoning. What is logic, Rose?' (pp. 37 and 38)

(Harmondsworth: Penguin 1977)

6. Charles Causley, Timothy Winters

Timothy Winters comes to school
With eyes as wide as a football pool,
Ears like bombs and teeth like splinters:
A blitz of a boy is Timothy Winters.

His belly is white, his neck is dark,
And his hair is an exclamation mark.
His clothes are enough to scare a crow
And through his britches the blue winds blow.

When teacher talks he won't hear a word
And he shoots down dead the arithmetic-bird,
He licks the patterns off his plate
And he's not even heard of the Welfare State.

Timothy Winters has bloody feet
And he lives in a house on Suez Street,
He sleeps in a sack on the kitchen floor
And they say there aren't boys like him any more.
Old Man Winters likes his beer
And his missus ran off with a bombardier,
Grandma sits in the grate with a gin
And Timothy's dosed with an aspirin.

The Welfare Worker lies awake
But the law's as tricky as a ten-foot snake,
So Timothy Winters drinks his cup
And slowly goes on growing up.

At Morning Prayers the Master helves
For children less fortunate than ourselves,
And the loudest response in the room is when
Timothy Winters roars 'Amen!'

So come one angel, come on ten:
Timothy Winters says 'Amen
Amen amen amen amen.'
Timothy Winters, Lord. Amen.

Collected Poems 1951–1975.
(London: Macmillan 1975, p. 77)

7. Barry Hines, Kes (1968)

[...] 'Teachers. They never think it might be their fault an' all.'
'No, I don't think many do, lad.'
'They think they're right every time. But there's sometimes when you can't help it, like this morning; an' like when you get thumped for not listenin' when it's dead boring. We', I mean, you can't help not listenin' when it's not interestin', can you, Sir?'
'No you can't, Casper.'
'You daren't say that to t'teachers though, they'd say, "Don't be insolent boy," smack!'
Billy stood up straight and waggled his head about, looking stern. Then he smacked the space between Mr Farthing and himself. Mr Farthing laughed out at his impersonation.

'That's what they'd say though, Sir.'

'I'm not saying it and I'm a teacher, aren't I?'

'Ar, well ...'

'Well what?'

'You do at least try to learn us summat, most o' t'others don't. They're not bothered about us, just because we're in 4C, you can tell, they talk to us like muck. They're allus callin' us idiots, an' numbskulls, an' cretins, an' looking at their watches to see how long it is to t'end o' t'lesson. They're fed up wi' us. We're fed up wi' them, then when there's any trouble, they pick on me 'cos I'm t'littlest.'

'They're not all like that, surely?'

'Most of 'em, Sir. An', anyway ... I can talk to you better than most folks.'

He looked down, blushing. Mr Farthing looked down at the top of his head.

'How are things at home these days?'

'All right, Sir. Same as usual I suppose.'

'What about the police? Have you been in trouble with them lately?'

'No, Sir.'

'Because you've reformed? Or because you haven't been caught?'

'I've reformed, Sir.'

Mr Farthing smiled at him. But Billy was serious.

'It's right, Sir, I haven't done owt for ages now! That's one o' t'reasons why MacDowall's allus pickin' on me, 'cos I don't knock about wi' their gang any more. An' it's since I stopped goin' wi' them that I stopped gettin' into trouble.'

'What happened, did you have an argument or something?'

'No, Sir, it wa' when I got my hawk. I got that interested in it that it seemed to take all my time up. It wa' summer then, you see, and I used to take it down our fields at nights. Then when t'dark nights came back, I never got back in wi' em. I wasn't bothered any more.'

'I try to get hold of falconry books an' read up about 'em now. [...] (pp. 82–83)

An' at home, if owt goes wrong on t'estate, police allus come to our house, even though I've done nowt for ages now. An' they don't believe a word I say! I feel like goin' out an' doin' summat just to spite 'em sometimes.'

'Never mind lad; it'll be all right.'

'Ar, it will that.'

'Just think, you'll be leaving school in a few weeks, starting your first job, meeting fresh people. That's something to look forward to, isn't it?'

Billy looked past him without replying.

'Have you got a job yet?'

'No, Sir. I've to see t'youth employment bloke this afternoon.'

'What kind of job are you after?'

'I'm not bothered. Owt'll do me.'

'You'll try to get something that interests you though?'

'I shan't have much choice shall I? I shall have to take what they've got.'

'I thought you'd have been looking forward to leaving.'

'I'm not bothered.'

'I thought you didn't like school.'

'I don't, but that don't mean that I'll like work, does it? Still, I'll get paid for not liking it, that's one thing.'

'Yes. Yes, I suppose it is.' (p. 84)

(Harmondsworth: Penguin 1982)

8. Walt Whitman, When I Heard the Learn'd Astronomer (1865)

When I heard the learn'd astronomer,
When the proofs, the figures, were ranged in columns before me,
When I was shown the charts and diagrams, to add, divide, and measure them,
When I sitting heard the astronomer where he lectured with much applause in the lecture-room,
How soon unaccountable I became tired and sick,
Till rising and gliding out I wander'd off by myself,
In the mystical moist night-air, and from time to time,
Look'd up in perfect silence at the stars.

Leaves of Grass, edited by Harold W. Blodgett/Scully Bradley.
(New York: University Press 1965, p. 271)

CENTURY THEATRE PRESENTS
EDUCATING RITA
BY WILLY RUSSELL
Sponsored by
BRS Northern
BRS Northern
MACBETH
BLAKE

FRANK........................DAVID SAVILE
RITA..........MARGI MACGREGOR
DIRECTED AND DESIGNED BY PAUL GIBSON
COSTUMES BY PAULA PATTERSON
LIGHTING BY ALAN NIELD
THE ACTION TAKES PLACE OVER THE FIRST YEAR OF AN OPEN UNIVERSITY COURSE
ACT ONE
SCENE ONE: JANUARY
SCENE TWO: FEBRUARY
SCENE THREE: MARCH
SCENE FOUR: APRIL
SCENE FIVE: APRIL
SCENE SIX: APRIL
SCENE SEVEN: MAY
SCENE EIGHT: MAY
ACT TWO
SCENE ONE: SEPTEMBER
SCENE TWO: SEPTEMBER
SCENE THREE: OCTOBER
SCENE FOUR: OCTOBER
SCENE FIVE: NOVEMBER
SCENE SIX: NOVEMBER
SCENE SEVEN: DECEMBER
THERE WILL BE ONE INTERVAL
FIRST PERFORMANCE
ROTHERHAM CIVIC THEATRE
ON
TUESDAY, NOVEMBER 15th 1983
THE PLAY WAS FIRST PERFORMED AT THE WAREHOUSE, LONDON, BY THE ROYAL SHAKESPEARE COMPANY ON JUNE 10th 1980, AND SUBSEQUENTLY AT THE PICCADILLY THEATRE, LONDON.
PRODUCTION PHOTOGRAPHS BY GERRY MURRAY

Acknowledgements

Non-Fictional Texts

Zu 1 From *Lern Yerself Scouse, How to talk proper in Liverpool,* volume 1, by Frank Shaw

Zu 2 From *The Pygmalion Factor,* by John Honey. Faber & Faber, London 1989.

Zu 3 From a leaflet distributed by the Open University and an article from *Rheinische Post.* Reprinted with kind permission.

Zu 5 From *The Mail on Sunday,* October, 12, 1988. By kind permission of PANDIS, München.

Zu 6 From *The Daily Telegraph,* July 16, 1984. (c) Telegraph Group Limited, London 1984.

Zu 10 From *Newsweek,* December 19, 1983. (c) Newsweek, Inc. All rights reserved. Reprinted with permission.

Zu 11 From *CBC (Canadian Broadcasting Corporation),* Toronto 1988.

Fictional Texts (excerpts)

Zu 1 From *Pygmalion* by Bernard Shaw. By kind permission of The Society of Authors on behalf of the Bernard Shaw Estate.

Zu 2 From Arnold Wesker's *Roots,* in *The Wesker Triology.* By kind permission of Jonathan Cape Ltd.

Zu 5 From *The Prime of Miss Jean Brodie* by Muriel Spark. Reprinted with permission. (c) 1961 by Copyright Administration Limited.

Zu 6 From *Collected Poems* by Charles Causley. By kind permission of David Higham Associates Limited.

Zu 7 From *Kes* by Barry Hines. By kind permission of Michael Joseph Ltd.

Cartoon by Edmund Busso: From a leaflet of the *Century Theatre,* Keswick, Cumbria. Reprinted with kind permission.

Photographs

S. 54, 61, 78 Rita (Julie Walters) and Dr. Frank Bryant (Michael Caine) in the film version of "Educating Rita".
Warner Brothers Film GmbH, München.

S. 95, 101 Willy Russell. By kind permission of the author.

The editor and publishers are grateful to the authors, publishers and others who have given permission for the use of copyright material identified in the text. It has not been possible to identify the sources of all the material used and in such cases the publishers welcome information from copyright owners.

987 654 32